The Culture Is I-God

God & Earth

The Culture Is I God
Introduction

There is no disclaimer in this book because the reader will learn that we are all responsible for our perception and interpretation of anything and everything we experience. I do not intend to disclaim anything I write or say. Maybe what I tell you will allow you to change your mind about how you want to conduct your affairs from now on. Anyone reading these pages is wise enough to follow one's own counsel and therefore acknowledges that I cannot do and will not tell anyone what to do. Peace!

"Men must want to do things out of their own innermost drives. Every civilization depends upon the quality of the individuals it produces. If you over organize the Nation over legalize them suppress their urge to greatness they cannot work and their civilization, order and or the nation shall collapses."

Sovereignty

Sovereignty is not something you sign up for, it is not an exclusive club you join but rather, it is a way you choose to experience life. It is a state of mind. True sovereignty begins with your choice to be free, to be self-reliant and to take responsibility for your own actions.

You are born sovereign and then as you enter into various contracts, and private agreements, you unknowingly give up your sovereignty, little by little, until one day you wake up and realize you are a slave. Therefore, stop accepting government issued benefits, or any so-called benefits that come with a hook to ensnare you into servitude and dependency and begin to reclaim your natural rights.

Strive to become financially independent. Get out of debt and stay out. Use your creative potential to make money instead of borrowing it from dishonest bankers. If it means lowering your standard of living temporarily so you can start living within your means, that will free your mind to be more creative and eventually help you to achieve a higher and more fulfilling standard.

I really encourage you to become self-employed. Follow your passions, express your uniqueness in the marketplace and you will have the potential to make more money than you ever made and having more time to spend on more important things in life. When you have more than enough money to support yourself and your family, without being a slave to an employer, or a bank, then you will have obtained financial sovereignty.

With adequate finances at your disposal you can be free to travel virtually anywhere on the planet, if you so choose. If a war breaks out, or if a conflict occurs, or say you are stuck in a natural disaster, you simply move away to some place else that is more accommodating. If you do not like the weather, with adequate finances you can chase your favorite seasons around the world.

For example, it is summer in the Southern Hemisphere when it is winter in the Northern Hemisphere. On the other hand, you can choose a variety of tropical destinations to go to year round. Freedom to choose your own weather is what I call climatic sovereignty.

Learn a second language or multiple languages get second citizenship, expand to multiple nationalities and residencies, explore the world, make it your playground, and achieve global sovereignty.

When you stop relying on doctors to heal you and begin to get in touch with your own body you can learn to boost your immune system so your body can heal itself, then you will have achieved health sovereignty.

This may be a new concept for some people, but you do have a choice. Sickness starts as a disease of the emotional body or energy body, which exists outside the physical body as an energy distortion or blockage, and then if not dealt with will eventually manifest as a physical aliment, and if still not dealt with may become a chronic or terminal condition. If you have a bad attitude about life, don't manage stress very well, and have lots of unresolved emotional issues then your immune system will be more taxed and your body more likely to be in a state of disease.

Therefore, your health is your responsibility and once you fully decide to make it such, you will no longer be a sucker for the pharmaceutical companies who really have no desire to cure you of anything; and why should they when it is your responsibility to begin with.

Another important area is energy dependency. If you are like most people you have been lead to believe that you must run your car on gasoline or diesel, that you must buy electricity from the power company, and you must use heating oil, propane, or natural gas to heat your home. Once again, dependency on these fuels makes you a slave to them. Many viable alternatives already exist that you can employee to gain greater energy independence or energy sovereignty.

When you stop relying on others to tell you how to have a relationship with God when you can go direct to God by whatever means you choose, without dogma, or power games, then that my friend is spiritual sovereignty.

Overall, sovereignty can take on many different shapes and sizes, but understand that sovereignty is not something you achieve once, only to forget about later like hanging a college diploma on your wall to collect dust.

Sovereignty is a daily practice and ongoing responsibility of the highest magnitude. Every choice you make will help you foster greater sovereignty or greater servitude. This realization will help you to be miles ahead of the game as restrictions on your liberties increase to the degree that someday you won't be able to use the toilet without first asking permission from the European.

So consider this: What will you do when the day comes that in order to buy food, fuel, medicine, see a doctor, borrow money, open a bank account, enter a federal building, board an airplane, train or cruise ship, etc., that your identity won't first have to be verified through your driver's license Federal ID (your social security account number) a retina scan, and eventually a clever little microchip (that will be implanted under your skin). For convenience and easy tracking, of course, it does not come to that if you and the majority of everybody else simply says no and becomes more self-reliant.

Your well-being, your freedom, your sovereignty, and your very future are your responsibility and it comes about by the choices you make starting today, not next week or next year. It must start today!

On this website www.ancientorderoffreeasiatics.com are alternative resources that can help you reclaim your sovereignty in a variety of ways. I recommend that you look through the various pages and when you feel a feeling in your gut about an item (an impulse) that is a message that you are on target to reclaim that aspect of your sovereignty.

These resources will act as tools to assist you. Nevertheless, know that only you can reclaim your sovereignty, nobody else can do it for you. Keeping that in mind, I encourage you to choose the highest path for your own well-being, and it is my sincere hopes that one or more of the resources we offer will help you to obtain the level of sovereignty you are looking for and/or need.

The Five Percent Nation

The Five Percent Nation is a nation within a nation, an organization created by Father Allah between 1964 - 1969, (Father Allah left the NOI in 1962 and in "63" some of the first borne are lifted up, by 1964 there are 500 young Five Percent).

The group's military structure and young members has prompted the South Carolina Department of Corrections to label the group a "security threat," and treat it as a "gang." Because of their affiliation with the Five Percent Nation, about 60 South Carolina inmates have been in solitary confinement for the past 7 year. They are only allowed 5 hours of exercise a week, but the service makes them stay in handcuffs and leg chains, they also only receive limited visits per month.

Where the Department of Corrections sees a threat, Five Percent see persecution. Inmates in lock-down have filed suit in the U.S. District Court against prison administrators, including the DOC. A Director ordered the lockup of 300 inmates a week after riots rocked a Correctional Facility. Inmates rioted and took hostages after the director implemented a policy forbidding long hair and beards (religious men in Hebrew cultures and Islamic cultures have Locks and Beards).

The Director said that because a few rioters were associated with the Five Percent Nation the Department placed 300 suspected members in lock-down across the state. Those who have been released had to convince officials that they were never of the Five Percent or renounce their culture by signing a form. The plaintiffs represented by the ACLU and Southern Center for Human Rights say they were not involved in the riots and claim they are in lock-down indefinitely because they refused to sign a paper renouncing their Culture/Creed.

"Due to the harsh conditions of solitary confinement, prisoners signed renunciation forms" after being confined in solitary for nearly a year. (DOC) has also banned all Five Percent literature, some prisons forbid the writings of Elijah Muhammed. While the Five Percent do claim scripture unique to their culture, followers often read the Holy Qur'an and/or Bible.

The Department's policy manual requires that a report of rules violation be completed for every inmate placed in solitary. The Federal Bureau of Prisons initially said that the group was considered a 'gang', but later amended that comment to "security-threat group." They are not a significant management concern for us at this time. Does the government track inmates based on their culture, can they be track according to behavior and conduct? The federal prison system reserves judgment as to whether the Five Percent are members of a 'gang' or not.

Georgia's Department of Corrections has paid closer attention to its group of Men that are Five Percent, but does not treat them as a 'gang'. 'We're sort of watching them as if they are a loosely affiliated, group of people with similar interests', as stated by DOC. This group that causes corrections departments to split hairs over terms like "gang" and "religion" was founded in 1964 by 'Father Allah' (who the Muslims called Clarence 13X Smith) after he left the Nation of Islam in 1962.

Born Clarence Smith in 1928, he moved to Harlem from Virginia in 1946 and joined the NOI several years later. He worshipped at Temple No. 7, then under the leadership of Malcolm X, was a gifted speaker and rose quickly to the position of Minister. When Clarence 13X left the NOI in 1962, he took the lessons of the WD Fard and Elijah Muhammed to the streets of New York City. The Five Percent remains very closely linked to the teachings of Father Allah.

The Father added to Elijah's teachings, reasoning that the collective Asiatic Blackman is God. The Culture is I God, the Power is truth and peace is the universal greeting and way of life of The Gods and Earths. Thanks to Father Allah's close relationship with Mayor John Lindsey, in 1967 the Five Percent leased a prime piece of Harlem property from the city with a lease of 99 years. The Allah School in Mecca still serves as The Five Percent headquarters. Unknown assailants killed Father Allah two years after Allah School in Mecca was opened, but some of the Five Percent believe city police were behind the plot.

Father Allah taught that once a man achieved mastery of self, he became a God, to the extent that he controlled his own destiny. Five Percent men refer to themselves as Gods and women as Earths, and the culture is 'I God'.

Five Percent teach Supreme Mathematics, Supreme Alphabet, a system devised by Father Allah wherein each letter or numeral denotes mathematical equations with an accompanying answer. "A" stands for Allah, "B" is Be or Born, "C" is See and so on.

For example, the 14th degree of the Supreme Alphabet "N" stands for Now Nation (End), and begins something like this, now is the time for the knowledge of self for the original man to wake up and come into the realization of his self as God, which is his true Self, or end in a pit of ignorance. The Father's wisdom was delivered in a "rapping rhythm" that elevated the New York City male youth to Gods. The Gods are trained to deliver their science, and the group has won converts by the hundreds. Today the group numbers in the thousands in the United States and over seas.

In an environment where a bowel movement is a public event and every request a power struggle, adherence to a ideology that defines the collective Asiatic Man as God is a political act, a manner in which to register protests against the institutions of the system, by following the master Father Allah. There are, no doubt, some Gods who joined The Five Percent for free knowledge wisdom and understanding of God and man. The movement tends to flourish in environments of impoverishment and decay because the message speaks directly to the disenchanted.

By the seventies, the Five Percent had become part of the American inner city experience, and 10 years later the group had organized meetings on the West Coast from Seattle to Mexico. Rap artists like Rakim, Big Daddy Kane and La'kiim Shabazz have used the Five Percent flag on album covers and have written lyrics influenced by 120 degrees. The Five Percent continues to be dominated by young adherents. Part of the allure is that there is no leader but Allah and the group's meetings, called parliaments, generally occur in public places. Some members of the NOI were once Five Percent, according to the (N.O.I.).

The group has been viewed as one of the most threatening 'gang' by the system because they are young and win converts preaching racial consciousness with a potent inner-city jargon. While Five Percent are Nationalists, they do not preach violence. Bilal Allah noted in an article, "The task at hand is to maintain one's own righteous existence while teaching others to be righteous. We place major emphasis on being articulate and well read." What constitutes a legitimate religion, culture or creed?

1) Q: Where Are The Five Percent (5%)?
Some are located in the Ghettos of Hell, the educational system, law enforcement, penal institutions, and high Government offices in the United States of America.

2) Q: What Nationality Are The Five Percent?
They look like you and I. Some are in high society, some are dressed poorly, but all are ether Asiatic or European.

3) Q: When Will They Make Them-Selves Known To The World?
They are making themselves known every day through their people, mostly the deaf, dumb, and blind whom the so-called righteous have not taught for they have failed to do their duty, which is to teach the uncivilized. There is a punishment for such actions, which the people will inflict upon them for not telling the truth, the truth that was taught to them, through the Messenger of Almighty God.

4) Q: How Will This Punishment Come About?
Through a mental and physical fight throughout the land, with all persons places and things on the planet earth but mostly in North America.

5) Q: Where Will Most Of This Fighting Take Place?
Most of this bloodshed will take place South East, North East, and South West. The West will be the fountain of dripping blood, insanity, murder, rape, and 85% total violence.

6) Q: How Will Most Of The Righteous Survive?
The only ones to survive this catastrophe will be the 5% who have taken upon them selves to learn, and listen. The 5% are the poor righteous teachers. The 5% are righteous to the degree of and between 85% and 10%. They have enough knowledge wisdom to control themselves and make up for the 10% and/or the 85% of unrighteousness' lacking in them. Hell is built upon imperfection, or it would not be considered Hell. Things are only right to a certain extent, due to the people who constructed it, having imperfect capabilities.

7) Q: How Can We Survive This Hell That Is Due Soon To Break Loose?
Survival is through different aspects of light that has been given out; in the form of knowledge, wisdom and understanding the light has been given to fit any and all occasions that would prevail itself at any given time; to recognize different segments of time as it has been given to man. If one fails to recognize it before it is upon you, it is one's own fault. There is no amount of pity given out, only total suffering when the time has been appointed, this happens individually and collectively due to certain circumstances prevailing in the United States of America.

8) Q: What Should The Brothers In The Wilderness Of North America Do To Counteract This Downfall That Waits?

As the Messenger of the Creator has taught, one should study lessons, read the Holy Books, so says Almighty God. Keep the company of the righteous, brothers who are trying to sustain them self in Islam, Hebrew, Coptic and/or any of the many cultures or creeds of earth. Most of all Asiatics who will teach Asiatics who are lacking in knowledge, and wisdom so says Almighty God. This is the time for all single brothers who have not continued themselves on through their seed, to merge and enjoin with a woman; come together with one another so says Almighty God Himself, for surely one will find it very difficult from here on.

9) Q: Where Is This Knowledge Wisdom And Light That Is So Needed?

There isn't any more light to be given; it is incumbent upon each individual to find and search for what he or she does not have, for surely the time is not far off.

Kwame Toure

Stokely Carmichael, Asiatic Blackman, Died a Hero in Africa, a Civil rights Leader, Father and Son. The fiery leader who coined the slogan 'Black Power' was 57 when he returned to the essence he lived in Africa for at least 25 years of his life.

Kwame Toure, who as the fiery political activist named Stokely Carmichael, was a seminal figure in the Black Power movement of the 1960s, died at the age of 57.

He died of 'prostate cancer' at his home in the West African Nation of Guinea, where he had lived since '1969', said Sharon Sobukwe, a Philadelphia-based member of Toure's 'All-African People's Revolutionary Party'.

Toure came to public attention at a time of great upheaval in America. First as a University Student and then as a Leader of the Student Nonviolent Coordinating Committee, he traveled frequently to the South to register Black People to vote. He registered thousands but paid a price, being arrested more than 21 times for his efforts. He once spent 50 days in Mississippi's infamous Parchman Penitentiary, where he was routinely beaten. It was during a protest march in Mississippi in June 1966 that he used the phrase 'Black Power'.

Toure and other Asiatic Black Leaders were continuing a march from Memphis to Jackson that had been started by James Meredith, who integrated the University of Mississippi. They joined the 'Walk against Fear' after Meredith was shot along a Mississippi highway.

Toure had been arrested as the marchers approached Greenwood, Miss. After posting bond, he returned to his colleagues and told them clearly that it was time to demand Black Power.

According to witnesses, he asked the marchers what they wanted and the response was 'Black Power'! The chants continued, and it became a rallying cry that galvanized pride among many Black People (African-American).

Nevertheless, the slogan was troubling to many in the civil rights movement, including the Rev. Martin Luther King Jr. He called the phrase 'an unfortunate choice of words'. Some whites who had supported the goals of integration viewed it as a 'call for racism in reverse'.

Some critics charged that Toure's rhetoric, which accelerated in tone after the Mississippi march, fueled rioting in cities across America in the next few years.

Toure tried to explain the term in the book 'Black Power', published in 1967 with Charles V. Hamilton, a Columbia University political science professor.

'It is a call for Black People in this country to begin to define their own goals, to lead their own organizations, to resist the racist institutions and values of this society'.

However, Toure's call for 'Black Power' was for too many in the civil rights movement more harmful than helpful because of the views from the church. For months, there was debate about what the phrase really meant, and many believe that debate helped splinter the civil rights movement. Earlier that year, He would always compare his views on violence with those of M.L. King, who advocated nonviolence in attaining civil rights.

'We had one simple definition that separated us', Toure said. 'He saw nonviolence as a principle, which means it had to be used at all times, under all conditions. I saw it as a tactic. If it was working, I would use it; if it isn't working, I'm picking up guns because I want my freedom by any means necessary'.

Toure was born in Port-of-Spain, Trinidad (Tobago) on June 29, 1941. His father was a carpenter, and his parents, with two of their daughters, traveled to the US. Toure remained in Trinidad, living with two aunts and his Grandmother. He received a traditional British education, and in an interview later complained that he was forced in class to memorize Kipling's 'White Man's Burden'.

In 1952 at the age of 11, he joined his parents in the Harlem section of New York where his father held a second job as a cabdriver to help support his wife, Mae, and children. The family moved to Morris Park, a European neighborhood in the Bronx, and for a time Toure belonged to the Morris Park Dukes, a local gang. Upon entering the prestigious Bronx High School of Science, he changed.

'I broke from the Dukes', he recalled in a Life magazine interview some years ago. 'They were reading comic books while I was trying to dig Darwin and Marx'.

Tall, handsome, stylish, he cut a dashing figure in school where he was popular with his classmates, both black and white. In 1960, after seeing pictures of Black People sitting in at lunch counters in the South, Toure became politically active. He rejected scholarships from several predominantly white colleges and entered Howard University in Washington.

During his first year, he took part in freedom rides, integrated bus trips to the South to challenged segregated interstate travel. In 1964, graduating with a bachelor's degree in philosophy, he became an organizer for the Student Nonviolent Coordinating Committee eventually rising to head the civil rights organization. He became the group's most influential and powerful leader and was instrumental in altering its orientation from peaceful integration to 'black liberation'. Toure resigned as chair of the organization in May 1967 and became affiliated with the Original 'Black Panthers', founded by Huey P. Newton and Bobby Seale. He became the party's prime minister.

However, he became disenchanted with the Panthers, apparently over Eldridge Cleaver's belief that coalitions could be formed with liberal whites. He quit the party and, in an open letter, charged that the party had become "dogmatic" in its ideology.

He left the United States in 1969 with his South African-born wife, singer and political activist Miriam Makeba, to live in Guinea, which he had visited in 1967. He changed his name to Kwame Toure, taken from Kwame Nkrumah, who is regarded by many as the father of Pan-Africans, and Ahmed Sekou Toure, the leader of Guinea. He founded the All-African People's Revolutionary Party, and by 1971, he was advocating a homeland in Africa for oppressed Black People.

'The Blackman should no longer be thinking of transforming American Society', He told Jonathan Power, a freelance journalist, who interviewed him in Conakry, Guinea. 'We should be concerned with Mother Africa. America is an Octopus with tentacles all over the world', he said. 'If the tentacles that grip Vietnam, South America and Africa are cut, it will be so much easier to rise up and cut off the head'. He continued to live in Africa in the ensuing years, making periodic trips to the US to see friends and lecture on the merits of Socialism, while criticizing Capitalism, Zionism and the US. Early in 1996, tests revealed that Toure had prostate cancer. He entered Columbia-Presbyterian Medical Center, where he received treatment including radiation therapy. He continued to receive treatment in the US and Cuba for the disease. Toure was twice married, once to Makeba and once to Malyatou Barry. Both marriages ended in divorce. His mother, Sister and two Sons, survived him. The Rev. Jesse Jackson, who visited Toure several times, in Guinea, stated that 'Toure was one from our generation who was determined to give his life to transforming America and Africa. He was committed to ending racial apartheid in this country (US). He also had a great hand in helping to bring those walls down on race in America'.

'The Key'

Man continues to be an economic and social slave because of his lack of knowledge, wisdom and understanding of law, history and science. Let there be light for knowledge is born equality. Light is required to lead man to necessary truths of science, law and history. The truth of science and history has been covered up by the use of mythology, theology, races and nations. 'The truth needs not, to apologize'. The ceremonies in Masonry are descended from the time of Solomon's Temple. Masons use the biblical legends about the temple in their stories and lessons, which they inherited from the building guilds.

Back in the middle Ages, in Europe, the Bible was available only in Latin; stories from the Bible were acted out in church to teach the biblical lessons to the common people. At first, the priests acted out the stories, but over time, the various trades and guilds became responsible for acting out particular legends. The masons had as their part the legends of the building of Solomon's Temple, and eventually they worked it into their own Lodge ceremonies as well.

The ceremonies of Masonry came from three sources, the Masonic guilds of England, the philosophies that were current when modern Masonry was getting started (1717, the date of the first modern 'grand lodge') and the Hermetic writings that came from North African, Byzantine, and Asiatic sources, also being discovered by European philosophers and scholars in Africa, decades before the founding of modern Masonry. These three sources are tangled up, which is why there were so many Masonic histories written for so many years. All of those sources had connections or contact with ceremonial traditions from King Solomon's Temple.

The Great Pyramids are the Emblems
Of the Asiatic Nation all 4,400,000,000

It requires only a small book to explain the truth of science, history, law, psychology, sociology, mathematics etc. However, it requires a very large book to cover up the truth of science and/or history by using Mythology, Theology, Isms, Race, and Fiction. (See Forbidden History by J. Douglas Kenyon)

The Black men, women and children continue to be economic and social slaves, because of a lack of the knowledge of their true history and the science they used all over the world. The Great Pyramids of Gaza was built by Khufu a great Asiatic builder. (See Black man of Nile and his family by Dr Ben)

In Scottish Rite Masonry, the question is asked: 'what is the meaning of the two pyramids on your left? Egypt, where the sciences first took their rise', 'To a Masonic judge, the triangle is figured for the pyramids, which planted firmly as the everlasting hills and accurately adjusted to the four cardinal points, firm and unshaken as they are, when our feet are planted upon the solid truth'. The infinite divisibility of the triangle, teaches the infinity of the Universe, of time, of space and of Deity, as do the lines that are diverging from the common centre ever increase their distance from each other, as they are prolonged infinitely. There is not enough religious doctrine and/or mystical wine in this world, or the next to make a man with knowledge of self drunk, open your eyes people of Earth, stop killing nature.

The fallen sons and daughters of the Asiatic Nation need to learn to love instead of hate and to know of their higher self and lower self. This is the uniting of the tribes and families, for teaching and instructing all families of the planet earth, and in the universe.

The two keys for civilization are in the hands of the Asiatic Nations (Earthlings). The Asiatic Nations who are descended from the Ancient children of the sun, whom founded on (Earth), Asia, Amexem, Atlantis and Mu, they are the Ancient Gods and their children are called Asiatic, Shabazz, Moabites, Cushite, etc., they are the founders of all ancient cities, the Ancient Egyptians, also the Hamitites and Mizriamites, also children from the Arabian seed of Hagar.

The Ancient Hindus, Nipponese, and Chinese, are the descendants as are Canaanites, Hittites and Moabites from the land of Canaan, the Asiatic Black Nations and Countries in North, South and Central America the Mexicans, Brazilians, Argentineans, Chileans, Columbians, Nicaraguans and the natives of San Salvador. The Ancient Turks are also the descendants of Hagar, who were the chief protectors of the Universal Creed of Man in the time of Monk Monk. (See J.A. Rogers Sex and Race)

Dedication

I dedicate this book to the thinkers and doers of Earth, because the masses of earthlings have become functional illiterates, due to the education system of today, it will be extremely hard, if not impossible, for a lot of people to understand these books and other books of truths that the people of earth have died for, they will have to become thinkers and reeducate themselves in history and the culture of the people who follow the laws of the universe. Anyone reading this book has to understand that words are given specific meanings in law. One such case is the word 'OF'; in most dictionaries, it has 18 meanings, depending on how you use it. In its most used form, it means belonging to or possessive. There is only one thing to remember, that is, you cannot use the meaning of words that you use in everyday conversation and apply them to any law for they do not mean the same thing in law. Failure to heed this warning, no matter what your mind thinks will put you back in the same situation that you are trying to get out from under; the usurpers have you believe their definitions through syntax. This book will attempt to show you how people in power, in order to gain control over the masses, and destroy their unalienable rights that are protected by the peaceful laws of the universe helped the lower self of man to deceived the higher self of man the world over. The illusion of freedom on Earth exists but the world today is less free than the world of just 120 years ago. **(Americans still have more freedom than most of the world)**

The men who founded the nations today would consider the people of earth virtual slaves. Some people who read this book and became frustrated with their lower self because they understand something is wrong, and believe the legal system of the world is crazy, should help the ones who can not see what man is doing to man. I cannot fault you for what the educational system has done to a lot of people, making a lot of us functionally illiterate, many have 5,000,000.00 in cash, others have little to eat their short life, however, when you know in your heart that something is wrong and you continue to gripe without doing anything about it, stop, and help the next form of life you see, or you deserve what you get, to give in to the power of your lower self! This book brings out just a small tip of the iceberg yet the truth is one, earthlings need water, we have higher and lower forms of life on earth, therefore, if the earth is hurt then man should help her by first helping him-self. This is just to start you off.

All aspects or degrees of life derived from mathematics, from mind to matter, from matter to mind. The Mind manifested nine cycles or nine aspects of life, from one to nine then from nine back to one, thereby adding a cipher to the knowledge to show its completion of a cycle. The mathematics from knowledge to born, are presently called supreme mathematics by the sons of men, which means all within mathematics are to be found within the son of man.

The Asiatics in North America are Gods & Earths; their Ancient ancestors are the Ancient Moabites, Cushiest, Hamites and Canaanites etc., who sojourned from the land of Canaan seeking new homes. That inhabited the North, Central, South and Western shores of the Americas; see the book Before the Mayflower.

Specific clarification needs to be given in the proper definition of class codes used by the Government the world over. We must understand that, as it is with all things under the guidance of man, changes occur to better update or extirpate the original meaning. It is on this wise that I give you the explanation that brought about race identification. The English continued the practice and enforced this system of caste, making it appear that there are not different races of people, but rather two distinct classes of nationals mainly European and Asiatic.

The following are the four classes that are the ethnology result of our present day Negro, Indian, Creole, etc, The Ab-original natives of the land mass called America held the first rank. They were the Asiatic people too; however, because of a royal decree ratified under the Emperor Charles V, the Asiatics (Blacks) were classified as Spaniards.

Thus, the Spaniards became legally ranked as first inhabitants. The second rank was Creole. These were the descendants, of the early European colonists, who were disowned by the English aristocracy because they claimed to be free men, based upon the Magna Carta. The third rank was a Mulatto; this was a mixture or amalgamation of European and Asiatics. The Mulatto was then barred from producing offspring from any other stock other than European. This created a different group, not ranked, called Mestizo; the fourth and final rank was called Indian. This was the product of amalgamation between the Mestizo stock and the Moors, which produced the reddish brown shade.

The changing of racial names became an easy task once the proper ranks had been designated. Since the Asiatics (Blacks) had become Spaniard, the amalgamation process for a different shade of Spaniard had taking place in Nova Spain. The Asiatic Africans and the Asiatic (Black) Spaniards were given a new name and a different rank. Later on, The Europeans took the Latin Spanish word for Black, Niger 'Negro' to be that new name and ranked this new Moor as fifth. Thus, the explanation for the 3/5 of all other persons that applied to the Negro in the Constitution for the US of A in that day and time.

Creole replaced Mulatto because it now meant 'descendants of Europeans' then the Europeans replaced the Spaniards as first class citizens. The establishment for the new order of races had begun. The Europeans declared and believed that their understanding was favorable in the eyes of God (Annuit Coeptis) and that this was the new order of the ages (Novus Ordo Seclorum). The (Asiatics) have a similar history to the so-called American Indians (their true names are not Indians, for you are what your fore fathers were) the Tribes from Alaska to Chile. There were as the Europeans called them; Civilized Tribes of Indians and there were Recognized Tribes of Moors. The American Indian tribes were the Cherokee, Chaloklowa, Chickasaws, Choctaw, Muskogee etc, etc, etc, The Asiatic tribes are 'Al, Ali, Bey, Dey Shabazz, Allah and El' etc, all of these original people lived in America 50,000 years before the European traveled to the Americas. In 1526, the Moors of Spain, were conquered by the Europeans and ordered to abandon their native dress and to assume the hats and clothes of the European-Christians, to renounce their language, their customs and ceremonies even their very names also to speak Spanish and behave Spanish and rename themselves Spaniards, some did, others rebelled and were later expelled from the country.

Manasses/King-Manasseh is the lost tribe, see: (1 K 8:16, 21:1-26, 2 K 21:1-8, 2 Ch 33:1-20) this lost tribe comprise the Asiatic people the world over also their children. Most of these divided people seem to be in idolatry, yet love God, worshippers under a fig tree and teach science, mysticism and/or mythology, most are under a creed of religion.

They oppose the Universal science of the sky but point to it, and the signs of the Zodiac and/or Jewels because of their beliefs, mythology, religion, and/or idol god worship in any of its forms. The truth needs no apology so fear you not. If you are not ready for the truth, close this book and do not read any further.

KNOWLEDGE
Chapter 1

Knowledge of the truth is a wise man's cipher, for you shall know the truth and the truth will make you free. All the evidence points towards the facts, that had the truth been taught in the schools of yesterday, there would have not been a need for the great statement to be recorded in literature named after the son of man Yeheshua, 'You shall know the truth and the truth shall set you free'. I am aware of the fact that the category of Astrology, Global Geography and the history of the Asiatic Nation (African-American), will conflict with nine out of every ten people of the US especially those often referred to as Negroes, Blacks and African Americans ranging between 45 and 60 years of age, owing to the educational system. Therefore, I concede that the category of science mentioned would appeal to the youth of tomorrow, those who will approach the ages of 18 to 29 by 2019. The restoration of civilization relies upon the ability of this group during the next 170 years of global, economic and social revolution.

The majority of those now ranging between 20 and 50 years of age have been too deeply instilled with emotional doctrines and distorted history, which has been written by, prejudiced educators during the past 379 years as of 1964. This group emotionally relies upon that which they have been taught to believe; facts and testimony are not the foundation of their faith, except in rare cases. These people accept, without question the beliefs of those among whom they are born and reared between and will disbelieve, even the evidences of their senses rather than disband with the impractical emotional beliefs, which have grown in them. People, who possess the applied knowledge of Mathematics, always employ the terms such as, science, truth and facts, rather than the religious terms bread only in false fear, mental conflicting opinions and secret hatred. Astrologers are aware of the fact that religious terms breed mystery, confusion, mental slavery, hatred, jealousy, dissociation, disorganize discrimination, caste system, economic and social degradation, warfare, bloodshed, destruction and starvation. Today religious worshippers have proven to the entire world that they would rather resort to emotional human hatred, fighting, and then suffer and die over the name of a mystery GOD and religion. Then to agree with simplified and applied truth facts or science involving their economic and social stride as shown in the 12 signs of the zodiac, look to the heavens all the truth is there, my word is bond. The song of numbers to the universe, suns, planets and triple darkness, for darkness is the limit of space, under and back of the universe of time, space and change is ever to be found.

The three-qubalistical veils of the (o-+) existence
000. AIN, Ain, Triple Darkness
00. AIN SVP, Ain Soph, the limitless
0. AIN SVP AVR, Ain Soph Aur, the limitless light
Chapter 2

1
KETHER

3
BINAH

2
HOKMAH

(DA'AT)

5
GEBURAH

4
HESED

6
TIFERET

7
NEZAH

8
HOD

9
YESOD

10
MALKUTH

In all current works upon the Kabala (Kabbalah), therefore, being copied from older works, we find emanation 2-4-7 constituting the Tree of Good (These words good and evil are not in the same meaning as man sees them but of the knowledge of good and evil not the act it self), 3-5-8 the Tree of Evil, and 1-6-9-10 the Tree of Life, the Shekinah, or Pillar of Mildness. The correct diagram are given supra, where it will be seen as it should be, the even, or esoteric, numbers 2-4-8 constitute the right-hand Pillar of Goodness, and the exoteric numbers 3-5-7 constitute the left-hand Pillar of Evil. In addition, it will be seen that the necessary planetary correspondences to each of the emanations when arranged in the latter manner will place benefic planets on the Tree of Good and malefic planets on the Tree of Evil.

Remember the definitions of the seventh emanation and the eighth emanations have been switched, they should read as such. The Seventh emanation is Netzach, meaning Splendor, and symbolizing God or infinity one of the perfect numbers, while the Eighth emanation is Hod, meaning Victory and symbolizing, He or Her, Man or Woman, the foot of the Tree of Good.

God, Himself, is both Father and Mother just as man has the male gene Y and the female gene X. The word Elohim, translated in Genesis as God, is Feminine plural Masculin Single; but the European translators of the Bible, not wishing women to share in anything Divine, have rendered it throughout in the Masculine singular. There is, however, an inadvertent admission of the Father-Mother principle when Adam is said to have been made in the image of Elohim, Male and Female made He them (XY). Hebrew scholars from the Chezz Nation of Hebrew Asiatic Blackman say that Eloh is feminine plural, and that the ending Im, is a termination of the masculine plural, the two being used together to indicate a feminine potency united to a masculine idea therefore they are Angles or Asiatics from knowledge to born in the Kabbalah and then you see both of this in man on the 10th degree Malkuth. Throughout the Kabala the Ancient of Days, is considered both male and female, and the Ten Emanations are divided into 3 positive, 4 neutral 3 negative attributes.

WISDOM OF THE KABBALAH
Chapter 2

This seems the proper place to point out that the unwritten kabbalah, like the written kabbalah, is set forth in symbolical language, with purposeful blinds and subterfuges to confuse the uninitiated; so that of the few who undoubtedly exist at the present day who have received it. Most remain in as much ignorance of its true interpretation, as the majority of students do after studying the more accessible written kabbalah. The unwritten kabala has been transmitted only through certain schools, of thought and science. The practical kabbalah treats of ceremonial magic, and includes the making of magic circles, wands, swords and pentacles, and the use of inscriptions and symbols for performing wonders. Accessible books treating of this subject (supra) are the 6th, 7th, 8th, 9th & 10th Books of Moses, The Greater Keys of Solomon the King, and The Lesser Keys of King Solomon.

The literal kabala is so written that the letters, numbers, and words must be transposed to perceive the meaning. It is a work really written in code, and must be systematically decoded to have any value. The code that must be used to decipher it, takes three different forms as follows: GEMATRIA, TEMURA, and NOTARIQUON or the DOGMATIC KABBALAH; this division has four chief headings; Sephir Yetzirah, Sephir Sephiroth, Asch Metzareph and The Zohar.

It was first taught by, IHVH to his selected angels who formed many schools. After the fall, the doctrine was communicated to man that by its means, he might regain his lost estate, according to tradition; it was handed down through an unbroken line of (Iseu) succession that included David and Solomon, to the time of the destruction of the second temple; when, for the first time, it was committed in writing.

This kabbalistic knowledge was a teaching concerning the origin of the Universe, Man's proper relation to IHVH and all other entities. Why man entered, material conditions? Moreover, how he might partake of the Tree of Good and Evil and how he ultimately regains his spiritual estate. Also partake of the Tree of Life, and so attain SELF-CONSCIOUS-IMMORTALITY. This information was handed down by word of mouth, as allegorical stories, thus it came to be an essential part of the wisdom for which the ancient lands of Atlantis and Mu are renowned.

The Tree of Life

The First emanation is called Kether, the Crown and symbolizing Life or Knowledge. It is the head of the Tree of Life containing the Male (Y) and Female (X) potencies.

The Second emanation is Chocmah, meaning Wisdom the head of the Tree of Good.

The Third emanation is Binah, meaning Understanding, being the head of the Tree of Evil.

The Fourth emanation is Chesed, meaning Culture or Freedom, being the Middle of the Tree of Good.

The Fifth emanation is Geburah, meaning Power or Refinement, the Middle of the Tree of Evil.

The Sixth emanation is Tiphareth, meaning Equality, Beauty, Attraction the Middle of the Tree of Life, where all influences join in a common harmonious Union.

The Seventh emanation is Netzach, Splendor, Beneficent, and Merciful the foot of the Tree of Evil.

The Eighth emanation is Hod, meaning Build or Destroy and Conflict, the foot of the Tree of Good.

The Ninth emanation is Yesod, meaning Born and symbolizing Formation, which gives external expression to Tiphareth, is next to the foot to the Tree of Life.

The Tenth emanation is Malkuth, symbolizing Asiatic or Knowledge added on to a Cipher. The Ideals of Kether, have been attracted by Tiphareth, and having undergone formative gestation of Yesod, are brought forth in full Virility, of expression, becoming in man SELF-CONSCIOUS-IMMORTALITY, the foot of the Tree of Life.

The Four Realms or four Kabbalistic worlds

Atziluth the celestial realm and the element fire, Briah, is Creation the spiritual realm and the element air. Yetzirah is Formation of the astral realm and the element water. Assiah is the realm of Action and symbolizing the physical realm and the element earth.

The first three emanations are related to Celestial Realms, even as Pluto, Neptune and Uranus have an influence over the highest ideals of man.

The second three emanations pertain to Jupiter, Saturn and Venus who have an influence over man's moral nature, reflective powers and his affections.

The third emanations, is reflective of Mercury, Mars and the Moon who have an influence over man's genius.

The final emanation the Physical world, practical action, as the Sun vitalizes and brings forth from the soil innumerable forms of life, or what has been perceived on the inner plane through extrasensory perception resides in the unconscious mind as a memory.

The word Kabbalah signifies traditional Knowledge. It thus refers to the Oral Law, as handed down from antiquity; and embraces the occult traditions of all lands and all peoples. The sacred books of the world include the Avesta, the Vedas, Bible, Qur'an and Zohar. In the Kabalistic system, each Hebrew letter is not only a number but in addition represents an idea.

The three mother letters are Aleph, Mem, and Shin. Aleph = the plane of spirit, Mem = the astral world, and Shin = the physical where all is given form. There are 7 active planets and 7 active attributes in nature so are there 7 double letters, Beth, Gimel, Daleth, Caph, Pe, Resh, and Tau. As there are 12 active Zodiacal signs and 12 active Jewels, so there are 12 single letters, although in detail they do not correspond to them: He, Vau, Zain, Cheth, Teth, Jod, Lamed, Nun, Sameck, Ayin, Tzaddi and Quoph. The Hebrew, Chaldeans, Arabic and Egyptian letters are very similar in vibration and numeric value. Kabbalistic is one of the universal standards or rules of measurement for the letters of the alphabet, and Astrology is the culture of the Asiatic Nation, in the wilderness of North America. The Asiatic Nation founded the universal order of Islam in Europe in the year 711 Anno Domini, and reeducated the confused human family of Europe. They in turn established the greatest civilization that the world would ever know.

The Asiatics taught the science of the number line or 3, 6, 9, 12, and the 60 seconds of the minute, the 60 minutes of the hour and the letters of the Alphabets, all this comprise some of the things that the cultured Asiatics taught in Europe. These Asiatics are the fore fathers of the so-called Negro in the Americas, who the Christians referred to in their literature as Negro's, Coons, Colored, Afro, Black, African and/or Heathen.

Elijah sits under the Juniper-tree, and weeps, Jesus was forsaken in Gethsemane, and Muhammed is forsaken in Mecca. These Prophets were happy at heart; but the Creator is great, and the Devil is like a Neophyte to his perfection. Say: 'God is one'. This I obey for a thousand and one times a night for one thousand nights, I did affirm the Unity of one. Night only means Light; and Unity and God are one or 1=34. Allah Understands the Culture or 1=34, also 7 or 77 or 777. For the Night will cover everything for light and dark are the same, six and five are the numbers of Adonai, the Holy Guardian Angel. The moon is the path of Gimel leading to Tiphareth and on to Kether.

The number 51 means power and knowledge, and its subject is appropriately equality, 49 is the square of seven also 26 when you look at God. This is why man hungers for the infinite, but he is not even ready for the finite, thus shall he devour the finite, and become the infinite, for he has become greedier than the shark, he must overcome all law, all nature and become him-self or 19. The number 31 refers to the Hebrew word LA, which means 'not'.

Blood and virginity have always been the most acceptable offerings to all the gods, but especially the Christian God, because such sacrifices come under the Great Law of the Rosy Cross, the giving up of the individuality, as has been explained. This is from the Adept Chamber of the Ancient Order of Free Asiatics from the Books the Kabbalah Unveiled, General Principles of Kabbalah and The Book of Splendor (Peace). The Exoteric Qabalah is a shell of that perfect fruit of the Tree of Life.

For the student unacquainted with the Qabalah we recommend the study of Supreme Mathematics and Supreme Alphabets from Father Allah the Founder of the 5% Nation, and The Zohar, the Qabalah is exotericism and literalism. The literal Qabalah is divided into three parts: GMTRIA, Gematria; NVTRIQVN, Notariqon; and ThMVRH, Temura.

Gematria is based on the relative numerical values of words. Words of similar numerical values are considered explanatory of each other, and this theory is extended to phrases. Thus in Hebrew the letter Shin, is 300, and is equivalent to the number obtained by adding up the numerical values of the letters of the words (RVCh ALHIM) Ruach Elohim, the spirit of Elohim and it is therefore a symbol of the spirit of Elohim. For R=200, V=6, Ch=8, A=1, L=30, H=5, I=10, M=40, total = 300. Similarly, the words in English Allah and One, each = 34, for A=1, l=12, l=12, a=1, h=8, and O=15 n=14 e=5 the total of each word is 34. (Knowledge = 96) Again, in Hebrew the name of the angel (MTTRVN) Metatron or Methraton, and the name of the Deity, (ShDI) Shaddai, each make 314; so the one is taken as symbolical of the other. The angel Metatron is said to have been the conductor of the children of Israel through the wilderness, of whom God says, 'My name is in him'.

With regard to Gematria the same can be said in phrases (Gen. 49:10), (IBA, ShILH) or (Yeba, Shiloh) in English 'until Shiloh come'= 358, which is the numeration of the word (MShICh) Messiah. Thus also the passage, (Gen. 18:2) (VHNH, ShLShH) Vehenna, Shalisha, 'And lo, three men stood by him', equals in numerical value (ALV, MIKAL, GBRIAL, VRPAL) Elo, Mikhael, Gabriel, Ve-Raphael, 'These are Mikhael, Gabriel and Raphael', for each phrase=701. I think these instances will suffice to make clear the nature of Gematria. Notariqon is derived from the Latin word notarius, a shorthand writer. Of Notariqon, there are two forms, in the first every letter of a word is taken from the initial or abbreviation of another word, so that from the letters of every word a sentence may be formed. (King Now Cipher Wisdom Lord Equality Divine God Equality) The kings nation is 360 and he is wise as the lord, to be = with the Divine God on Earth or 110 in 120 also to teach all families of Earth.

Thus in Hebrew every letter of the word in (BRAShITH) Berashith, is made the initial of a word, and we obtain (BRAShITh, RAH, ALHIM, ShIQBLV, IShRAL, ThVRH) Berashith, Rahi, Elohim, Sheyequebelo, Israel, Torah; 'In the beginning Elohim saw that Israel would accept the law'. As in Knowledge = Knowledge, Now, Cipher, Wisdom, Lord, Equality, Divine, God, Equality. The second form of Notariqon is the exact reverse of the first. By this the initials or finals, or both, or the medial, of a sentence, are taken to form a word or words. Thus the Qabalah is called (ChKMH, NSThRH) Chokhmah, Nesethrah, 'the secret wisdom' and if we take the initials of these two words Ch and N, Chen, 'grace'. Similarly, from the initials and finals of the words (MI, IOLH, LNV, HShMIMH) Mi, Iaulah, Leno, Ha-Shamayimah, Who shall go up for us to heaven? (Deut. 30:12), are formed (MILH) Milah, 'circumcision' and IHVH, the Tetragrammaton, implying that God hath ordained circumcision as the way to heaven. Temura is permutation. According to certain rules, one letter is substituted for another letter preceding or following it in the alphabet and thus from one word another word of very different orthography may be formed. Thus the alphabet is bent exactly in half, in the middle, and one half is put over the other, and then by changing alternately the first letter or the first two letters at the beginning of the second line, twenty-two commutations are produced. These are called the Table of the combinations of (TzIRVP) Tziruph.

For example's sake, I will give the method called (ALBTh) Albath, thus:

11	10	9	8	7	6	5	4	3	2	1
K	I	T	Ch	Z	V	H	D	G	B	A
M	N	S	O	P	Tz	Q	R	Sh	Th	L

Each method takes its name from the first two pairs composing it, the system of pairs of letters being the groundwork of the whole, as either letter in a pair is substituted for the other letter.

Thus, by Albath, from RVCh, Ruach, is formed DTzO, Detzau. The names of the other twenty-one methods are : ABGTh, AGDTh, ADBG, AHBD, AVBH, AZBV, AChBZ, ATBCh, AIBT, AKBI, ALBK, AMBL, ANBM, ASBN, AOBS, APBO, ATzBP, AQSTz, ARBQ, AShBR, and AThBSh. To these must be added the modes ABGD and ALBM. Then comes the Rational Table of Tziruph, another set of twenty-two combinations. There are also three Tables of the Commutations, known respectively as the Right, the Averse, and the Irregular. To make any of these, a square, containing 484 squares, should be made, and the letters written in. For the Right Table write the alphabet across from right to left in the second row of squares do the same, but begin with B and end with A, in the third begin with G and end with B, and so on. For the Averse Table write the alphabet from right to left backwards, beginning with Th and ending with A, in the second row begin with Sh and end with Th, etc. The Irregular Table would take too long to describe. Besides all these, there is the method called (ThShRQ) Thashraq, which is simply writing a word backwards. There is one more form called the Qabbalah of the Nine Chambers or (AIQ BKR) Aiq, Bekar. It is thus formed:

300	30	3	200	20	2	100	10	I
Sh	L	G	R	K	B	Q	I	A
600	60	6	500	50	5	400	40	4
M final	S	V	K final	N	H	Th	M	D
900	90	9	800	80	8	700	70	7
Tz final	Tz	T	P final	P	Ch	N final	O	Z

I have put the numeration of each letter above to show the affinity between the letters in each chamber. Sometimes this is used as a cipher, by taking the portions of the figure to show the letters they contain, putting one point for the first letter, two for the second, etc. Thus, the right angle, containing (AIQ) will answer for the letter Q if it has three dots or points within it. Again, a square will answer for H, N, or K final, according to whether it has one, two, or three points respectively placed within it. So also with regard to the other letters, there are many other ways of employing the Qabalah of the Nine Chambers, which I have not space to describe. I will merely mention as an example, that by the mode of Temura called (AThBSh) Athbash, is found that in (Jeremiah 25:26) the word (ShShK) She'shakh, symbolizes BBL, Babel. In order that you might readily knowledge the wisdom, to bring about an understanding to the contents of this lesson, you are advised to lay aside all that was taught you so you can see which is to know, this is mathematics. As a result, you will be guided by common reason rather than by traditional emotional belief. I am aware of the fact that religious teachers have a monopoly on a mystery God, but they do not have this same hold on mathematics, the science of geometry involving the 12 signs of the zodiac, or the universal law called, I self lord and master.

UNDERSTANDING
ASTROLOGY AND ASTRONOMY
Chapter 3

The difference between Astrology and Astronomy is that Astrology teaches about the Asiatic people's characteristics, talents, actions and reactions, also sociology, economics and global geography or space and time. Astrology is the science of the influence of the heavenly bodies as they affect the nations and groups of people, land, sun, moon and stars. Astrology is about the person or people, sun, moon and stars. It is the stairway leading into the deeper self of man and woman. In Astronomy, the same principles apply to all the stars, suns, planets and moons, differing in manifestation because of size, motion, density and relative place. The earth floats in the midst of a vortex, the outer extremity of which is somewhat beyond the moon, the vortex is globular corresponding to the form of the earth. Some vortex or globular are not closed at the end for some are open at both ends.

The vortex (whirlpool in space = motion + mass) turns the earth on its axis, with its own axial motion. The 'outer part of the vortex has a greater velocity than near the earth's surface, which has an axial motion of one thousand miles an hour'. The moon has a 'vortex' surrounding it, which has a 'rotation axially once a month'; being an open vortex the moon does not turn. If a vortex 'does not have contact with a planet then it is called a dead planet. From the swiftest part of the earth's vortex, its force is toward the earth's center, if the earth were not present, the vortex 'would make another one', and the vortex is the foundation of the planets. Things in space and or the Atmosphere do not fall to the earth because of magnetism, but they are 'driven toward the center of the vortex', by the power of the solar space vortex. The Prophets taught that the vortex formed the earth as a ball of fire, and by this same power is the warmth of the surface of the earth manufactured to this day, heat does not come from the sun to the earth, and the schools teach the superstitions of the European, who believed all things, came from the sun. They also talk about the attraction or gravitation of the sun extending to other planets. If you cast water on a dusty floor and the drops of water will assume globular forms, the globular form is natural to a liquid, and it is cause by a power external to its self. If you approach one of the drops of water with a piece of cloth, the globe of water will climb up into the cloth. The water had no attraction for the cloth, or the cloth for the water. The power that accomplished this was external to both, and was the same as the vortex that brought the earth its center and maintained it therein, when the cloth approaches the drop of water it breaks the vortex and the water goes into divisible parts and on into the cloth, in search of the negative polarity. That which is a physical substance has length breadth and thickness, remains so by no power of its own but by the vortex. The Earth's vortex exist within the Sun's vortex, as the same goes for Mercury, Venus, Mars, Ceres, Jupiter, Saturn, Uranus, Neptune Pluto, Chiron, Xenia and 53 objects in the Kuiper Belt and the combination of all these vortexes within the Sun's vortex is known by the name, solar system. Were the Sun planet extinct, the vortex would instantly make another Sun.

Nether light, nor heat, nor attraction of gravitation comes from the sun to the earth. Heat decreases in force in proportion to the square of the distance from the place of generation.

Though a man sees the light of the sun, that which is light is the polarity of the physical sun in space caused by the lines of the sun's vortex. In experiments on earth, the flash requires a certain time to polarize these infinitesimal rays, and for convenience sake, such lapses of time are the travel of light. Daylight is not manifested by the sun or by the photosphere of the sun. Daylight is the condition of things polarized within the master vortex. The earth coming between the master's focus and the outer extreme manufactures night, so that night and day continues all the time and we realize them both alternately in consequence of the axial motion of the earth. As in the case of night or any darkness, when the substance of the atmosphere is disturbed in its polarity, as in an eclipse, there is no direct manifestation of the earth's vortex and such is the cause of darkness. For which reason nitrogenous plants grow rapidly at night, while the ripening of certain fruits and grains requires the light of day. Therefore, when man eats, breathes, and drinks water these elements go into dissolution and the heat is eliminated and lodges itself in man. For if, certain herbs pile together and they commence dissolution their heat is spontaneous combustion.

Wherein the Europeans have taught erroneously that heat comes from the sun, as may be proven that so-called heat is created at the expense of destroying something, which is called combustion. There is not anything in the universe that can give off forever without receiving a supply forever. Heat had to be stored up in the first place in all things in heaven or earth before it could be liberated. When a man burns a stick of wood, he can produce no more heat from it than what was already stored in it. Allowing the sun to be four and a half million miles in diameter, giving it fifty per cent of the burning capacity and it would be entirely consumed in eighty thousand years! To think that heat exists of it self is folly to suppose that heat can be produced forever without a supply is not supported by any fact in heaven or earth. Friction produces heat but it is because the abrasion liberates the stored up vortexes heat. The same errors concerning the light of the moon have been made. The superstitions of the Europeans still cling to the philosophers. Finding a coincidence in the tides with certain phases of the moon, they have erroneously attributed the cause of tides to the power of attraction in the moon manifesting on the ocean, which is taught to this day as sound philosophy. Attractions exist not in any physical substance as a separate thing. There are not any substance of attraction, or gravitation, these powers are the manifestation of the vortex. If the vortex is charged into a piece of steel, it is called a magnet, because it will draw its own kind to itself. When two pieces of steel, (one attracting the other) have been charged with the power of the vortex in proportion to their dimensions this is a magnetic force. If one of the pieces of steel is twice the size of the other, its magnetic force will be two times as powerful. The true form of a magnet to manifest the greatest positive and greatest negative force should be a triangle after the manner of a line of vortex from the equatorial surface of the earth to its center and then toward the North Pole. By having two or more with their poles together, a square is produced, which is now balanced within the emissions of the vortex.

By suspending a ball of magnetic iron along side a suspended cup of water, it will be discovered there is no magnetic attraction between them no more than between two cups of water, or between two vessels of clay.

Were there such things, as magnetic attraction between iron and water or between water and water, a still further discrepancy would result? Admitting the general parts of the moon as to iron and stone and clay and water, to be alike an un-alike unto the physical earth. The power of the magnetic attraction of the earth, as against the moon's to hold the tides from rising, would be in the ratio of the different sizes of the two bodies, and their respective distances from the water contended for. In which case there would be more than four thousand million times advantage of power in the earth, for if we give the same magnetic equivalent to each, we must give to each a decrease in proportion to the square of the distance of their centers from the point in contention.

The same philosophy holds concerning the sun and to Jupiter and Saturn and mars, and all other planets, making allowance for their different densities and velocities. As to the so-called attraction between two earth substances, as granite, sandstone, lead, gold, clay, and water, it is far less than between two steel magnets. Wherein, it has been observed that it is utterly impossible for any attractive force to exert from one planet to another, or even from a planet to its own satellite. Even if we use the most extravagant base of measurement on the sun, we will see this supposed attractive force, does not extend to the earth by more than seventy million miles, wherein they have taught an error in place of truth! The Christian Astronomers are the stargazers who go to heaven by way of an expensive telescope and promulgate that which they imagine live on the planets. Such philosophy cannot help solve our economic and social problems, the real sun, moon and stars dwell in the Asiatic family. Now you can draw your own conclusion as to the whys and facts of Astrology and Astronomy. Astrology erases all beliefs and opinions of superstition, confusion, religious mystery, false fear and idol or image worship.

Astrology has always involved this universal fact that God and Earth in the course of one second can manifest the sun moon and stars on the earth without employing a telescope. Therefore, man and woman comprise the supreme manifestation of the whole of creation space and time that need no doctrine of religious mystery fear and superstition, to influence them to employ that which is right. Because the science of Astrology, man woman child, fire, air, water, earth, and plants constitute the great force of creation often referred to in science as atomic energy or voltage, electromagnet and current. Remember the Asiatic body contains all the elements of nature; we are what we eat, drink, inhale and exhale. Therefore, all energy generates from prana and the power of the chakras, for man and Mind are one. The physical bodies of people are the only moving planets or heavenly bodies in our universe, people are planets, and every-thing is governed, by natural laws. Above and below, all obey those by which they manifest, and when these laws are un-comprehended, any phenomenon seems mysterious. Progression depends upon knowledge, progression must be founded on knowledge, only through knowledge of self can one expect to progress, all knowledge is based upon experience.

We send or go to objects by way of walking, riding, flying, sailing, observation, mathematics and vibrations. The universal code of facts perfection and the guidance of practical knowledge wisdom and understanding of life are comprised from one to nine and or from one to twenty-six; this is the understanding of life from the womb to the tomb. (See Green Books and/or Oahspe)

THE CODE OF THE ROMAN ORDER
Chapter 4

The Roman numerals (I, II, III, IV, V, VI, VII, VIII, IX, X, L, C, D, M, and M̲) and the Latin and/or Spanish languages comprised some of the Christian codes of which was born out of the Asiatic Universities in Span. Argentina, Brazil, Peru, Columbia, and Venezuela, comprised the springboard for the European Nations to have many different races and castes systems to populate the Americas, and to try and kill the original inhabitants of the Western hemisphere. In 45 BCE, New Year's Day is celebrated on January 1 for the first time in history as the Julian calendar takes effect. Soon after becoming Roman authoritarian, Julius Caesar decided that the traditional Roman calendar was in dire need of reform.

Introduced around the seventh century BCE, the Roman calendar attempted to follow the lunar cycle but frequently fell out of phase with the seasons. In addition, the Roman body charged with overseeing the calendar often abused its authority by adding days to extend political terms or interfere with elections. In designing his new calendar, Caesar enlisted the aid of an Alexandrian astronomer, who advised him to do away with the lunar cycle entirely and follow the solar year, as did the Egyptians. The year calculated to be 365 and 1/4 days, and Caesar added 67 days, making January 1 the first of year, rather than in mid March. He also decreed that every four years a day added to February, thus theoretically keeping his calendar from falling out of step. Shortly before his assassination in 44 B.C., he changed the name of the month Quintiles to Julius (July) after himself. Later, the month of Sextilis was renamed Augustus (August) after his successor. Celebration of New Year's Day in January fell out of practice during the Middle Ages, and even those who strictly adhered to the Julian calendar did not observe the New Year exactly on January 1. The reason for the latter was that Caesar and Sosigenes failed to calculate the correct value for the solar year as 365.242199 days, not 365.25 days. Thus, an 11-minute-a-year error added seven days by the year 1000, and 10 days by the mid-15th century. The Roman church became aware of this problem, and in the 1570, Pope Gregory XIII commissioned Jesuit astronomer Christopher Clavius to come up with a new calendar. In 1582, the Gregorian calendar, omitted 10 days for that year and establishing the new rule that only one of every four centennial years should be a leap year. Since then, people around the world have gathered en masse on January 1 to celebrate the arrival of the Gregorian New Year.

Rome

Traditionally founded by Romulus in 753 BCE, ruled by kings until the expulsion of Tarquin the Proud in 510 years before the christen era. By mid second century, Rome had subdued the all of Italy and her power brought her into conflict with Carthaginian interests in the western Mediterranean also taken place was the Hellenistic world in the east. Success in the Punic Wars gave Rome her first overseas possessions, and the Macedonian wars eventually left her dominant over Greece and much of Asia Minor.

Provincial unrest and dissatisfaction at home with the Senates control of command brought a series of ambitious military leaders to the fore-front in open rivalry, each able to count on the support of a devoted soldiery, until civil wars culminated in the defeat of Pompey by Julius Caesar. Caesar's brief dictatorship established the principle of personal autocracy, and after his assassination by republican conspirators, another round of civil war ended with Octavian's assumption of authority as a kind of constitutional monarch. The US comprises every so-called race of the European family; Rome enslaved the Europeans and Asiatics through false doctrine of religious mystery and image, or idol, worship of various mystical God phrases using pictures and idols. The earliest known natives of Italy are Asiatic, thus making the base of the Latin race Asiatic not European, Mr. D. Wilson based his observations on the earliest Etrurian pottery he refers to well known examples of Etruscan vases molded in the forms of Asiatics heads and of Greek pottery painted with the same characteristic features and woolly hair. 'Specimens of both are preserved among the collections of the British Museum' and furnish interesting evidence like, the permanency of the Asiatic, and the familiarity the Greek and Roman had with the Etruscan artists who had Asiatic features long prior to the Christian era. *(Asiatic = Mind and body of the Black people of Earth) (see J.A. Rogers Sex & Race) The term European implies the people who control the Board of Real Estate, Commerce, Production and Distribution in and under the umbrella for the Order of Roman (European) colonization, which manifested with Wall Street in Amsterdam or New York. Of which are the headquarters of the Nobles, Dukes, and Lords also Duchesses, the true jury over the wealth and culture of the American Nation. The forefathers of the Asiatic (Asiatic Nations) who were defeated by the Roman conquerors, after having undergone some 364 years of intermittent conflict from Patagonia to Alaska, Canada and Iceland. Having been defeated by the Roman tribes of South America, they submitted themselves to Roman slavery under names such as Negro and Indian, which resulted in the loss of their birthrights. In the Christian calendar 1774 is equivalent to 14,860 Asiatic calendar year, 1453 – 1492 Christian calendar year is equivalent to 14,539 – 14,578 Asiatic calendar year, the Moors ruled old Spain for 750 years therefore all of the tribes of Portugal, Spain, Italy and Sicily are of one family, namely Latin and Asiatic. The Roman conquerors subtracted 13,086 years and 3 months from the Asiatic calendar, to arrive at the Gregorian calendar. 1865 Christian calendar year is equivalent to 14,951 Asiatic calendar year, 1946 CCY is equivalent to 15,032 ACY. Once in fascist Italy, Benito Mussolini dreamed of reviving the glory of Rome and he looked to Africa for colonies to conquer. In 1935, Italy invaded Ethiopia; a proud nation that at one time symbolized the best of Africa.

WWII

In 1939, when World War II was declared, Nigerians were urged to support Britain in the name of a better postwar world, a world that would include democracy and self-determination. The USSR and the US, were speaking out against colonialism. In Britain, the Labor Party with its strong anti-imperialist views was coming to power. One of the party's leaders, C.R. Attlee, declared in the London Daily Herald. We in the Labor Party have always been conscious of the wrongs done by the European races to the races with darker skins.

We have always demanded that the freedom, which we claim for ourselves, should be extended to all men. I look for an ever-increasing measure of sovereignty in Africa.

In March 1945, the same session of the British Parliament that approved the Richards Constitution also passed these Ordinances, The Minerals Ordinance, the Public Lands Acquisition Ordinance, and the Crown Lands Ordinance. Two months later, 30,000 union members struck for 37 days in a general strike. Since the participating unions controlled vital services, such as rail services, the strike paralyzed much of the nation. In 1947, the British granted independence to India and Pakistan and appeared willing to grant independence also to Burma and Ceylon. Nineteen forty-eight became a turning point in Nigeria.

The Richards Constitution, approved in 1945, was supposed to be in effect for nine years. However, in 1948, the new governor, Sir John McPherson, announced intentions to revise the document and to recruit Nigerians into the senior ranks of the civil service. Admirers of Azikiwe had formed an assemblage called the Zikists. H.R. Abdallah, president of the movement, declared, 'I hate the Union Jack with all my heart because it divides the people wherever it goes. It is a symbol of persecution, of domination, a symbol of exploitation.

We have passed the age of petition, the age of resolution, the age of diplomacy. This is the age of action plain, blunt and positive action'. Ten Zikists leaders charged with sedition are arrested. By 1949, six European firms handled about 66 percent of Nigeria's imports and nearly 70 percent of her exports. In November 1949, a labor disturbance erupted in the Eastern Province and a police detachment opened fire on the striking miners, many of whom were killed or wounded. When protest swept across Nigeria, including a series of Zikists riots, the Zikists movement was declared illegal. In 1951, another constitution the McPherson Constitution endeavored to pacify Nigeria, without success. At this point, three major political parties had sprouted in Nigeria, each with a strong national base. In the East was the NCNC; in the West, the Action Party, called AG in the North, the Northern People's Congress or NPC. No party claimed a nationwide majority. The British government convened a constitutional conference in London, producing the Littleton Constitution of 1954. A federal election produced a coalition government between the NPC and NCNC that is, between the North and East.
In 1957, a constitutional review conference was called and a national government formed to prepare Nigeria for independence. The three regional parties the NPC, NCNC, and the AG joined under the leadership of Prime Minister Abubakar Tafawa Balewa. Federal elections were held, during the month of October 1, 1960, the Union Jack was lowered. The green and white flag of the Federation of Nigeria flew in its place. Nigeria had become a sovereign Confederation; three years later, Nigeria became a republic. In January 1966, the federal prime minister and other key political figures were assassinated in a military coup. A new government was declared the then head of the army, Major General Aguinyi Ironsi, quickly imprisoned the coup leaders. Within weeks, there was a coup within the army and Major General Aguinyi Ironsi was dead. On August 1, Colonel Yakubu Gowon, assumed the leadership of Nigeria. Gowon won over the West but tensions grew with the East.

When it was rumored that Israel and the US planned to back the East in a war against the rest of Nigeria, the North reacted with rage against its Ibo population, which had Eastern roots, estimates of Ibo dead range from 10,000 to 30,000, Estimates of those who fled to the East range from 600,000 to 2 million. A civil war existed between the North and the East. Secession was more than an emotional issue; it was also an economic one. Most of Nigeria's oil industry was located within the East or off its shores. For centuries, the East had been the poorest area of Nigeria but now it could become the wealthiest. On May 30, 1967, the East declared itself the Republic of Biafra.

The East anticipates that international oil companies would force their governments to support Biafra. Nevertheless, the United States was entangled in Vietnam; the Soviets were worried with quelling Czechoslovakia; and most European powers were wary of a conflict that other African Nations proclaimed to be an African matter. Britain was an exception. It supported Gowon's government the Federals against Biafra.

Near the outset of hostilities, the Federals imposed a massive blockade on the East, which kept out food, medicine, and essential goods. Meanwhile, war destroyed the harvest of the East. Each night on world news, audiences around the world saw the results: the unblinking eyes of children waiting to die; the pleas of a mother as she showed her starving newborn to the cameras; the hoards of flies coating the faces of those too weak to wave them away. At its peak, foreign observers estimated Biafra's death toll to be 30,000 a day.

Humanitarian organizations rushed food and medical supplies to Biafra but they were ineffective because of the corruption within the Biafra army and because of hindrance by the Federals. The Nigerian air force went so far as to shoot down a Red Cross DC 7 in broad daylight, claiming it was an accident due to mistaken identity. Britain continued to back the Federals with Maurice Foley, undersecretary of the Foreign Office, explaining, "We have links extending over 100 years, we have 16,000 people in Nigeria, great investments, and much trade of enormous mutual benefit to Nigerians and ourselves. We have no other honorable option." When the Soviets also extended aid to the Federals, Britain became even less likely to withdraw.

Ultimately, Biafra surrendered unconditionally. The war lasted longer than two and one-half years. There is no accurate record of how many died. On Independence Day, October 1, 1970, Gowon outlined a nine-point program for a new Nigeria. In 1975, he was overthrown in a bloodless coup. His successor, a Northern general, ruled for 201 days before being killed and replaced by the army's chief of staff. Nigeria was confounded under an unbalanced, persistent military rule. Finally, in October 1979, in the wake of a nationwide election, Nigeria returned to civilian rule. However, On December 31, 1983, the military seized power once again. Instability, elections, assassinations, labor protest, and accusations of corruption have continued. In 1985, a coup led by Major General Ibrahim Babangida brought a new government to power, along with the promise of a return to civilian rule.

GNOSTICS OCCULTISM
ANCIENT MASONRY
Chapter 5

The philosophy of Gnosticism was declared heretical by the early Roman Church, it is a religion that combines occultism, mysticism, astrology, magic, esoteric Hebrew, a modified Christian perspective of redemption also Zoroastrianism. Included also are the ancient rituals of Egypt and Mesopotamia that are prevalent in Free Masonry today. The Gnostics beliefs in resurrection and dualism come from the Zoroastrian religious ritualism.

(God created man and woman in His own image on the Sixth Day, giving them charge over the world; but Eve did not yet exist.) God had set Adam to name every beast, bird and other living thing. When they passed before him in pairs, male and female, Adam cried 'Every creature but I have a proper mate', I pray God will remedy this injustice. God then formed Lilith, the first woman, just as He had formed Adam, out of pure dust. From Adam's union with this woman, <u>Tubal Cain</u> and his sister sprang Asmodeus. Many generations later, Lilith came to Solomon's judgment seat.

Adam and Lilith never found peace together; for when he wished to lie with her, she took offence at the missionary position he demanded. "Why must I lie beneath you?" She asked! "I also was made from dust, and am therefore your equal." Because Adam tried to compel her obedience by force, Lilith, in a rage, uttered the magic name of God, rose into the air and left him. Adam complained to God: "I have been deserted by my helpmate." God at once sent three angels to fetch Lilith back. They found her beside the Red Sea, a region abounding in lascivious demons, to which she bore Lilim (The children of Lilith) at the rate of more than one hundred a day.

"Return to Adam without delay," the angels said, "or we will drown you!" Lilith asked, "How can I return to Adam and live like an honest housewife, after my stay beside the Red Sea?" "It will be death to refuse!" they answered. "How can I die," Lilith asked, "when God has ordered me to take charge of all newborn children: boys up to the eighth day of life, that of circumcision; girls up to the twentieth day. None the less, if ever I see your three names or likenesses displayed in an amulet above a newborn child, I promise to spare it." To this, they agreed; but God punished Lilith by making one hundred of her demon children perish daily; and she could not destroy a human infant, because of the angelic amulet. She escaped the curse of death, which overtook Adam, since they had parted long before the fall. Un-dismayed by the failure of Adam unable to keep a suitable helpmate, God again created a woman and let him watch while he built up her anatomy. The sight caused Adam such disgust that even when this woman, the First Eve, stood there in her full beauty, he felt an invincible repugnance, so then God took the First Eve away. Where she went, nobody knows.

God creates a third woman, having taken a rib from Adam's side in his sleep, He formed it into a woman; then adorned her, like a bride, with twenty-four pieces of jewellery, before waking him. (Some say that God created Eve not from Adam's rib, but from a tail ending which had been part of his body. God cut this off, and the stump-now a useless coccyx-is still carried by Adam's descendants.) According to Isaiah 34: 14-15, Lilith dwells among the desolate ruins in the Edomite Desert where satyrs (**se'ir**), reams, pelicans, owls, jackals, ostriches, arrow-snakes and kites keep her company.

The Gnostics were religious mystics who proclaimed gnosis, knowledge, as the way of salvation. They taught that to know your true self allowed Gnostic men and women to know God directly, without any need for the mediation of rabbis, priests, bishops, imams, or other religious officials.

Religious officials, who were not pleased with such freedom and independence, condemned the Gnostics as heretical and a threat to the well being and good order of organized religion. Gnostics sought knowledge and wisdom from many different sources, and they accepted insight wherever it could be found. Gnostics studied religious works from the Egyptians, Mesopotamians, Zoroastrians, Muslims, and Buddhists. All such sacred texts disclosed truths and were to be celebrated for their wisdom.

The Occult

The word occult means hidden forces and the art of subjecting such forces under man's control. (Everything is governed by natural laws). As above so below, all obey those by which they manifest. Man's progression must be founded on knowledge. Through knowledge of himself, can he expect to progress. All knowledge is based on experience, distinguishing the me from the not so me. No one can deny his or her own existence. Occult scientists have demonstrated Magic, Astrology and Alchemy. The occultist prepares for a immortal life, a life of never ending progression while yet gaining knowledge of universal laws.

Ancient Masonic Brethren

These rites and pictorial representations that have seemed significant to an important group of people the world over, of every Ancient Nation. Remnants have been found in remote shores of Africa, fertile valley of the Nile, Red Sea, Tigris and Euphrates rivers. Certainly the most enlightened inhabitants of our globe, this Divine symbolic language, which has successfully weathered nature.

The Ancient Doctrine preserved in the symbolic forms of Masonry, the rites and hieroglyphics that Albert Pike labored over to understand, also the teachings of Mackey come from the same foundation, the works of the first Masons who lived in the valley of the Euphrates and the Chaldeans will not be forgotten.

The original Masons were Magi, and or mental builders. The Masonic Brethren labored in the erection of Solomon's Temple. The early Mason was not a worker in stone, but a mental builder, astrology was studied as a sacred science, these were the magi, the original masons. From childhood a rigid, culture in the development in mental physical, spiritual faculties to penetrate the innermost recesses of nature. Therefore, the early masons sought out the correspondences in nature, and built their pictured symbols into the far reaches of the sky as the Temple of Solomon, for the Grand Architect of the Universe.

The Ancient Masons ever sought to find a fitting symbol to represent each principle, or function of life, and build this into a Temple. Why were two Pillars, erected in the Temple of Solomon the King? Life depends upon positive and negative forces, there being no life without sex. Realizing these two attributes they wisely erected two columns, the pillar on the right is called in Hebrew Joachim and the pillar on the left is called Boaz. The Masculine and Feminine symbol therefore is the Plumb a symbol of the masculine principle in nature, as is the earth being considered the womb of nature. The square is suited for measurement of plane surfaces, angles and single planes.

The Compass being an instrument used to draw circles, the union of the compass and the square form a diamond, the hardest and most precious of stones. With the G in the center as God, that manifest life represented by the Hebrew letters Yod-He-Vau-He or **IHVH** within the compass and square.

Modern Masonry had its beginning in the society of Architects under the protection of King Robert Bruce. The Order of Knights Templar trace their origin from the Ancient Mysteries practiced in the East but they only knew three degrees out of the 7 lesser and 10 greater, the doctrines of the old Egyptians that are, seven branches of astrology, seven branches of alchemy, seven branches of magic, seven psychic senses, seven physical senses and seven states of consciousness, all of which must be mastered before reaching adept-ship.

Jacques de Molay, a knight of eastern France the last to hold the honor of grand master of the Knights Templar. Initiated in 1265 at the age of twenty-one then at forty-eight he was grand master of the order.

On October 12, 1307, the grand master is among the nobility of Europe who acted as a pallbearer at the funeral of Princess Catherine, the deceased wife of King Philip's brother, Charles of Valois. For Friday the Thirteenth, would be the most unluckiest day of the year for the Order of the Temple as Philip's troops descended on every Templar commander over all of France and put fifteen thousand men into chains that had been made ready for them. All this on October 13 to the issuance of a papal bull on November 22, the imprisoned Templars' in France were being tortured to obtain confessions of heresy.

Thirty-six Templars' died in the first few days after the tortures began. To put to rest all thoughts that the Templars' were not actually guilty but victims of greed, it was decided to have the order's grand master make his confession before the world. The nobility, prelates of the church, and commoners were invited to witness the historic event on March 14, 1314 ace.

De Molay was to confess his guilt and that of the order, but Molay condemned himself to death in these words, 'I think it only right that at so solemn a moment when my life has so little time to run I should reveal the deception which has been practiced and speak up for the truth. Before heaven, earth, and all of you here as my witnesses, I admit that I am guilty of the grossest iniquity.

However, the iniquity is that I have lied in admitting the disgusting charges that lay against the Order. I declare, and I must declare, that the Order is innocent. Its purity and saintliness are beyond question. I have indeed confessed that the Order is guilty, but I have done so only to save myself from terrible tortures by saying what my enemies wished me to say. Other knights who have retracted their confessions have been led to the stake, yet the thought of dying is not so awful that I shall confess to foul crimes, which have never been committed. Life is offered to me, but at the price of infamy. At such a price, life is not worth having. I do not grieve that I must die if life can be bought only by piling one lie upon another'.

Brother de Charney shouted out his own retraction and assertion of the innocence of the order, as he and de Molay were hustled off the platform. While on fire, Jacques de Molay called down a curse on Philip of France and upon all of his family for thirteen generations. He called upon both king and pope to meet with him within the year for judgment at the throne of God. Clement V died in the following month of April, followed by Philip's death in November of the same year.

Ancient Masonry
'The Most Profound Secrets of Masonry Are Not Revealed In the Lodge They Belong Only To the Few'

'There are Masons, Mechanics and Carpenters, these are the first three degrees of Ancient Masonry, those who know will see that Ancient Masonry is very close to the Free Masonry of today'

The common gavel, 12-inch gauge and the 24-inch ruler are the tools of a Mason. '133 Psalm' is read in the Temple of Solomon in the first degree. The grip of the Ancient mason was a pressure of the thumb at the base of the others index finger in the dark to see another brother and or brothers. The grips name is Boaz after the husband of (Ruth 2:1). 'Unto Adam also and to his wife did the Lord God make lamb skin aprons, and clothed them'.

The Master '...who secured the Golden Fleece with the help of Medea and the Argonauts...' For the standard representing a Roman Eagle, is carried, by the head of each 'Roman' legion, Truth and Union, are the words, and you shall be cautious, using the listening ear, a silent tongue, and a faithful heart.

The Fellow Craft is opened on the number five, after they whom said unto them, say now Shib'bo-leth, and he said Sib'bo-leth, for they could not frame their mouth to pronounce it right, then they took them, and slew them at the passages of Jordan, and there fell at the time of the E'phra-mi-ites forty and two thousand, Judges 12:6. In this was manifested the love of IHVH toward us, because He sent his only begotten Son into the world that we might live through him, I John 4:9. Thus, he showed me and behold, the Lord stood upon a wall made by a plumb line, with a plumb line in his hand, Amos 7:7. In addition, he set up the pillars in the porch of the temple and he set up the right pillar, and called the name thereof Ja'chin and he set up the left pillar and called the name thereof Boaz 2 Chronicles 3:17. Jacob's ladder or the Theological Ladder is said to contain three principal rounds, denominated Faiths in IHVH, Hope for immortality and Charity for all in the Universe. There is a point within the circle, yet the circle is bounded on the east and west, the two perpendicular parallel lines, represent the anniversary of John the Baptist and John the Evangelist.

The Master in Ancient Masonry is Tubal Cain! He kneels before the altar on both naked knees, raises both hands to heaven with the arms bent, and gives the hailing sign. Saying 'Is there no help for the widow's son'? The sign of the degree shows where the hope lies for a Master Mason, this is made by drawing the right hand, palm down, from left to right across the abdomen in the region ruled by the sign Libra and letting it fall to the side. The pass-grip of an Ancient Mason is the right hand between the joints of the second and third fingers where they join the hand; its name is Tubal Cain the true Master of Masonry. The apron, in this degree, is worn with the triangle down over the square showing $3 + 4 = 7$. The Trowel is to spread the cement of brotherly love and affection, that cement which unites them into one sacred band or society of brothers, among whom no contention should ever exist, but that noble emulation of who can best work or best agree. Jubela, Jubelo and Jubelum, these names, are to let you see the light of the Ancient bother that was killed under number 3. We first learn of Enoch in Genesis 5, fore he is the grandfather of Noah. The sprig of cassia, the emblem of this degree is a pelican feeding her young, on one side of her a rose and on the left a sprig of cassia for immortality, nevertheless low six, and G marked on left breast or jewel are for the Ancient Mason to see his brother in the dark and also in the light.

Boaz, Ja'chin, Mah-Hah-Bone, (marrow of the bone or the lion's grip) all show that, Jubela strikes GMHA a blow across the throat with a 24-inch gauge, Jubelo gives GMHA a blow across the breast with a square, and Jubelum strikes the Master upon the forehead with a gavel, where upon the Master falls dead. In the words of King David 'Fear is to warn you of the danger not to make you afraid of it'. For you shall 'never underestimate your appoint' and 'never take what he offers you', If you must resort to violence then you have al-ready lost and if a battle cannot be won, do not fight it'.

Solomon said see the word of a master in the Ancient works of 'Tubal Cain'; (Gen 10:2) also the 'grips are the compasses'. The jewels of a Master are 'Friend ship, Morality and Brotherly Love', and are as strong as a 'lion's paw'. The Grand hailing sign is of distress, or the mourning for 'The Grand Master Hiram'. In the dark, the words 'O Lord, My God, is there no help for the widow's Son'? From an EA, to a FC, you are 'raising' your self on the square. In the first and second attempt there are failures to raise the body, then the grand hailing sign of distress is given, the words are, 'O Lord my God! '0' Lord my God! '0' Lord my God! I fear the Master's (Note: IHVH in the Qabalah) word is forever lost'. The three stages of man are youth, manhood, and old age, which were referred to as the 'The three steps on the Carpet'. Moreover, 'The pot of incense', is one of the symbols in the lecture to the 'Old Masters'. Because the bee is such an energetic insect, never appearing to rest from sun-up to sundown, as the world turns, the bee and, hence, the beehive have long been symbols of industry or work for man.

The book of constitutions guarded by the Tyler's sword is the general name applied to any book or even a MS., containing the fundamental law, regulations, or constitutions of a Masonic body or system of bodies. The sword pointing to a naked heart is a symbol in the Master's Degree and one of the eight hieroglyphical emblems.

The All Seeing Eye is naturally a symbol of watchfulness, having the connotation both of solicitude and of detection. The Anchor and Ark are emblems of a well-grounded hope, and a well-spent life. The hourglass is an emblem of the passage of time or the brevity of life. The scythe of Father Time, is the emblem of death, brought into the Master's Degree by the Ancients, not only in the symbol of the hourglass, but in the monument representing the virgin weeping and time standing at her back. The setting maul is a wooden hammer consisting of a mass of wood, either globular or barrel shaped and usually a long wooden handle for two-hand use, indeed the setting maul, coffin, and spade appeared in all Masonic charts as late as 1824 and are still illustrated in some Masonic monitors.

The EA degree treats the physical plane. The Master Mason degree treats the spiritual plane. The FC treats the astral plane. At the death of the physical body, both the physical form and the etheric body are lost. The physical body and the etheric body cannot exist on the astral plane. The sign of the FC is made by taking hold of the left breast with the right hand as though to tear a piece out of it, then the hand is drawn with the fingers partly closed quickly to the right and dropped to the side. The breast is the seat of emotion and the right breast indicates the higher aspirations and longings. The left breast symbolizes the more physical emotions; and as the region of the heart, ruled by the sun, is the center of vital life.

Ancient Masonry teaches that each soul is a responsible entity working out its own deliverance from a voluntary and purposeful incarceration in matter. On the higher astral plane man no longer eats organic substance to live he no longer eats his fellows, even a one cell animal is his lowly kin.

The 47th Problem of Euclid

While these principles are illustrated by numbers, geometry, and mathematical symbolism, the Tetragrammaton the operation of divine law is incorporated in to the understanding of this great mathematical symbol, the three sides represent the divine trinity, knowledge, wisdom and understanding. The Ark corresponds to the mundane houses, in the zodiacal signs and starry constellations of the universe for the physical body of man is the planet and he has an astral body and the ego is his mind.

The Book of Constitutions is symbolized by the oral law the same as 120 or 33.33 one third of 360. The long winding staircase refers to the annual journey of the sun, for there are 365 days in a year on earth, but only 360 degrees in the sun's annual cycle. Finally yet importantly, the master's grip is called the Lion's grip, because it is typical of the sun's action in the sign Leo where it exercises its most virile power. **(Love Truth, Peace, Freedom & Justice, or; 12, 20, 11, 4 & 10)**

CUBA
Chapter 6

Peru, Mexico, Isabella or Cuba, America, Canada and Alaska all of which comprise the land of the cultured Asiatics, the descendants from the Ancient Nations, (Red Sun) the Fathers of Civilization who inhabit and founded the planet earth. Thus, America lies in the geographical region of the Crest of Asia often referred to as The Temple of the Sun, Moon and Stars of which scientifically imply the greatest inclination of the earth axis to the Sun, during the months of June, July and August, in the Northern Hemisphere. What the ancestors, of this land namely Amexem or America is today without a doubt of contradiction, Original, Asiatic, Moor and/or Asiatics, this name Moor is derived from the name Moabite. The Crest of Asia symbolizes the Akhet Khufu, or Pyramid as shown on the reverse side of a *US* One Dollar Bill. Names such as Negro, Colored, Black, Afro American, African American, American Indian and Redman are slave labels of the Roman Cross Order of segregation, hatred, slavery and exploitation. The reconstruction period of 1853 thru 1865 resulted in the United Order of the Christian European world of organized labor, agriculture, industrial and commercial unionism and military procedure, which made the European Nations, the mistress of the Oceans. Railroads and factories were being built at a record pace, and the California gold rush was on. The slavery issue became more and more divisive among northern states. Franklin Pierce at this time was the President of the US, the 14th President. A former congressional representative and Senator from New Hampshire, he came into office a decade before the Civil War. Although his roots were in the Northern state of New Hampshire, Pierce sided with the South on the slavery issue.

Franklin Pierce approved the Gadsden Purchase in 1854; taking parts of Arizona and New Mexico from the Mexicans **(see the Mexican War of 1846)**, He also signed the Kansas Nebraska Act in 1854, which allowed voters in newly stolen territories to decide whether to permit the slavery of the Asiatics. Then Pierce tried unsuccessfully to purchase Cuba from Spain. '1854' also ushered in the era Manifest Destiny, a belief that territorial expansion of the US was inevitable. Franklin Pierce shared in the American expansionist fever, that made the US what it is today, a corporation.

With the election of Abraham Lincoln as US President in 1860 and the outbreak of the civil war shortly thereafter, Pierce became a bitter and outspoken opponent of both the Lincoln administration and the war. He spoke of the war as the "butchery of white men" for the sake of "inflicting" emancipation on slaves who did not want it.

From 1853 through 1990, nearly 225,000 attorneys had been admitted to practice before the bar of the Supreme Court. (What was that Jesus said about Lawyers?) No admissions records exist for the periods between 1853 and 1790 of the Bar. Why did some one remove them? Prior to 1925, no written applications were required for admission, and attorneys were admitted on an oral motion by bar members. Abraham Lincoln learned and practiced law before the admissions records existed; this is why he was such a good Lawyer.

During the world domination of the Asiatic Nation, the blond women of Pelan (an island situated on the Aegean Sea) and the blond women of Patagonia South America had manifested their cultured height in that society. Which qualified them to establish the society of the Cross (+), with mystery and emotional false doctrines, as a positive weapon of liberating themselves from the amalgamated iron handed rulers, or dictators, who had shielded the secrets of nature as shown in the signs of the Zodiac and established a doctrine of mystery and religious superstition by force.

As a result the following amalgamated generation of Asiatic Fathers and blond mothers, they grew up in ignorance of the science of the 12 signs of the Zodiac and the applied principles of Islam. By being under the influence of 13th century, Islam of variable unreasonable procedures of religious worship, strenuous mysterious prayers, and the restriction of literary education to the common masses was insufficient for them to see the light of God. The amalgamated rulers of the Muslim world converted the society of Islam into a regimentation, caste system, slavery, economic and social degradation, crime, bloodshed and destruction of life. From this was born the army of the mystic banner of the cross. In turn, they were led by militant pale women, supported by many wise Muslims, struggling for freedom, Moslem or Muslim, women and their children looking for freedom all of which resulted in some 364 years of intermittent conflict. A great battle between two different types of religions the crescent and the cross, or Muhummed and Christ. The period of crucifixion lynching, burning and murdering one another over ideas of impractical mysteries of variety, which has dominated the world for some 700 years and has manifested with the racial and color scheme of corruption, and should be over but, it is not.

The Muslims with their strenuous religious worship and superstitions are not guilty of the establishment of the race and color scheme. For they are guilty of the caste system and segregation, according to class and rank a method of mystic and/or superstitious religious worship in the institution called Mosque, from which was born the institution of worship. The Christians institution of worship is called the Church and the race and color scheme with its marriage license laws established by the blond women has men and women slaves to them selves.

This system at one time in history prohibited the issuance of a marriage license to Asiatic men and women who desired to marry European women and men in North America, especially in the US.

This is founded on the myth of the so-called Negro and so-called White people, blood, skin and physical shape of races, which was born out of the church system namely the Catholics, Protestants, Baptist and Jewish Synagogues.

During the colonial era, Native Americans were made to adopt the Spanish language and were converted to Roman Catholicism, the religion of the Spanish colonizers, at the time of the Spanish conquest in the early 1500s; numerous advanced Native American civilizations existed. The Spanish ultimately conquered the Asiatic Native American civilizations and extended their control over the entire region, calling it New Spain. Spaniards quickly intermarried with the indigenous people, producing a growing population of mixed European, Moors Patagonians and Asiatic Native American ancestry. When Columbus first landed on Cuba it was inhabited by the Ciboney, a tribe related to the Arawak. Colonization of the island began in 1511, when the Spanish soldier Diego Velázquez established the town of Baracoa. Velázquez founded several other settlements, including Havana in 1515. The Spanish transformed Cuba into a supply base for their expeditions to Mexico and Florida. Because of the savage treatment and the exploitation of the land and people, the aborigines became, nearly extinct, forcing the colonists to depend on imported African slaves for the operation of the mines and plantations.

During the year 1830, Spanish rule became even more repressive, provoking a widespread movement among the colonists for independence. In 1844, an uprising of African slaves was brutally suppressed. A movement during the years 1848 to 1851 for annexation of the island to the United States ended with the capture and execution of its leader, the Spanish-American general Narciso López. In 1868 freedom fighters under the leadership of Carlos Manuel de Céspedes proclaimed Cuban independence, during the Ten Year War, a truce was granted, granting many important concessions to the Cuban people. In 1886, slavery was abolished, and importation of cheap labor from China had ended by 1871. Two main indigenous groups existed in Argentina before the European arrived. In the northwest, near Bolivia and the Andes, was a people known as the Diaguita, while further south and to the east were the Guarani. The first Spaniard to land in Argentina, Juan de Solis, was killed in 1516, and several attempts to found Buenos Aires were stymied by the local inhabitants.

When the French captured Spain's King Ferdinand VII, Argentina fell completely under the rule of the local viceroyalty, which was highly unpopular. The locals rebelled against the viceroyalty and declared their allegiance in the year 1816.

The first Europeans were led by Ferdinand Magellan, who pioneered passage through the treacherous strait that now bears his name, his expedition named the mainland 'Tierra de los Patagones, spawning the legend of a race of Patagonian giants.

To the east of the Andes, the Patagonian pampa is an immense desert, among the five largest deserts in the world. West of the Andes both the Central Valley and the Coast Range have sunk into the Pacific; hot springs lay revealed by coastal erosion, while great glaciers fragment the landscape.

Florida was settled long before Europeans had discovered the peninsula. Native Americans had arrived in Florida 10,000 years before the first Europeans. European voyages of discovery began when Columbus discovered the islands of the so-called New World in 1492. Spanish exploration of Florida began in 1513 with expeditions near St. Augustine, the Florida Keys and Tampa.

French settlement of Florida began in 1562 as Huguenots, French Protestants, established them on the St. Johns River not far from the Spanish settlement at St. Augustine. This settlement was easily conquered by the Spanish, but Spain's early dominance of Florida was threatened over time by the expansion of English colonies from the north and French colonies from the west. By 1702, the English had sacked St. Augustine and, by 1719, the French had taken Pensacola. Americans joined the battles for Florida in 1803, following their purchase of Louisiana from the French. The history of Florida during this period is one of territorial gain and loss until 1821, when Spain ceded Florida to the United States of America. At the same time, European settlement and conflicts had a devastating effect on Native Americans and set the stage for the Seminole Wars. Spain crusaded for the conversion of Native Americans within its territory, often brutalizing populations that did not convert to Catholicism. The British in Georgia were no less in tolerant, rather than convert, the British chose to clear the native populations from so-called British territory. In 1750, Tribes of Creeks together with Moors migrated into Florida where they became known as the 'Seminoles'. The Spanish and Portuguese had a monopoly of the East Indies spice trade until destruction of the Spanish Armada in 1588, which permitted the British and Dutch to seek their share of this wealthy import business.

Native American

The number of so-called Indians killed out right by the Christians were three and a half million, and the other three million died out because of their treatment by the Christians.

Christianity has become a social and cultural movement as well as a religious belief and practice. When discussing Indians, most Europeans do not worry about facts.

An assault on a village of Deerfield Massachusetts by Indians in 1704 was labeled as a massacre, but an assault on a village of Cheyenne in 1864 was celebrated in Denver as a victory over hostiles. The US Supreme Court announced in the 1700 that Indians could not vote because they had neither been born in the United States of America nor naturalized.

Hollywood cast Italians to play Apaches, and then protest they meant no harm. In New England, groups of Algonquian peoples had inhabited the area for thousands of years. Their homelands stretched from Lake Champlain in the west to Maine's Atlantic coast and from the St. Lawrence Valley in Quebec to Northern Massachusetts.

The Sokokis on the middle and upper Connecticut River, the Cowasucks were up-top of the same river, Missisquois on the northern shore of Lake Champlain, the Pennacooks of New Hampshire's Merrimack Valley, the Pigwackets in the White Mountains, the Androscoggins of western Maine, and the Penobscots, Norridgewocks, Wawenocks, and Kennebecs farther east.

Knights of Columbus

The mind set of the Union of 1853 thru 1865 manifested the Knights of Columbus and the Ku Klux Klan of which involve some four million people of red or ruddy pale skin, with long hair. The Knights of Columbus initial meetings are not known to the public, the first public reference to the Order was on February 8, 1882.

Michael J. McGivney an Irish Jesuit priest founded the Knights of Columbus; the Order's principles were "Unity" and "Charity", the concepts of "Fraternity" and "Patriotism" were added later. The Connecticut legislatures granted a Charter to the Knights of Columbus, and formally establish the order as a Legal Corporation 1,882 years after the Christian era. This took place in New Haven, the Order's primary objective, was to dissuade Catholics from joining other secret societies by providing the Knights of Columbus. The K of C is Catholic men committed to the defense of the Priest-hood; they are unequivocal in their loyalty to the Jesuit Priest.

KLAN
Chapter 7

All non-Protestants, liberals, (if there is such a person) trade unionists, and striking workers are denounced as subversives by the Ku Klux Klan, the Klan was organized in Pulaski, Tennessee, during the winter of 1865 by six Confederate army officers who gave their organization this name from the Greek word Ku Klos or circle. Membership is open to so-called 'white Protestant males 16 years of age or older'; so-called 'Blacks, Moors, Roman Catholics, non-so-called whites and Jews are excluded'. The Klan is very active in many states such as Pennsylvania, New Jersey, Ohio, Indiana, Illinois, Georgia, Colorado, Oregon, Kansas and Oklahoma. In the early years, the Klan regarded the U.S. government as hostile and oppressive.

The Klan also believed that the so-called African-Americans are inferior and therefore shall not and will not be allowed to rise above the status of a slave. There was another group of Klansmen that held a secret convention in Nashville Tennessee in 1867 they adopted a declaration of loyalty to the US Constitution and the Government of America. The convention designated the Klan as an invisible empire, provided for a supreme official called the Grand Wizard of the Empire, assisted by ten genii. The next principal of the Klan is the Grand Dragon of the Realm, assisted by eight hydras; then there is the Titan of the Dominion, assisted by six furies; and the Grand Cyclops of the Den, assisted by two nighthawks.

In 1871, Congress passed the 14th Amendment to the US Constitution. In that same year, President Ulysses S. Grant issued a proclamation calling all illegal organizations to disarm and disband; thereafter hundreds of Klansmen were arrested. By 1915 in Georgia, a preacher, Colonel William Simmons, incorporated a new fraternal Order of the Klan. In 1920 the Order of Klan had expanded rapidly and became active in many states, during the 1930's the Ku Klux Klan remained active particularly against Trade Union Organizers. It also threatened so-called Blacks, Negroes, and/or Colored People if they tried to vote. In the 1940,'s the Klan joined with Nazi Germany and held large rallies in, NJ and GA., the US then revoked the Klan's Charter in 1947. After the US civil rights act of 1964, the Klan experienced an increase in membership, reaching an estimated 40,000 by 1965. In 1970, some Klan leaders ran for public offices in the South, amassing sizable numbers for the vote. There are about 15 organizations existing today in the US under the KKK, a former grand wizard of the Klan, David Duke was elected to the Louisiana House of Representatives in 1989 and ran in the gubernatorial election (1991).

Albert Pike held the office of Chief Justice of the KKK while he was simultaneously Sovereign Grand Commander of Scottish Rite Masonry in the Southern Jurisdiction, (the KKK was also known as the Invisible Empire of the South). In 1869, Forrest ordered the Empire to disband because of the extreme violence. 1,915 years after the Christian era, is marked as the rebirth of the KKK and by 1920; they controlled some states such as Indiana from the courthouse to the state house. Almost all of the top officials of the revived Klan were also so-called Masons, with 5 million members, also called them selves white Protestants, with several Senators and Governors. By 1944, the KKK collapsed, in a storm of corruption, murder, rape, and torture. Pike was not just any Freemason he was the head of the Supreme Council, which has defacto control of the entire worldwide Masonic movement. Therefore, the Ku Klux Klan was an official and planned organization with political overtones that foreknowingly was set up to engage in murder, arson, and blackmail to achieve the Klan's political objectives. The KKK and Freemasonry are as seamless as could be. From its inception through the open recruiting of European American Masons, in newspapers, to the use of Masonic Temples and halls for meetings, to the rituals, rites, and themes, to the high degree of Masonic membership of the leaders of the old and new Klan, even the present cover-up can be seen to be part of the Organized Klan. European American Freemasonry has continued their involvement with reactionary Politics; they have never stopped and have never given up the mission to stop the so-called Black man from 'moving on up'.

Many have speculated on what happened to the millions of members that were on the rolls up to the final downfall at the hands of the IRS in the 1940. We now know they simply carried on inside the Masonic lodges as if nothing had changed at all. What really had changed? In most regions of the country, the local KKK Tavern membership was indistinguishable from the local 'Blue' Masonic lodge membership, there are whole lodges of them, after all the KKK had openly advertised in newspapers for new recruits specifying that 'Masons were preferred'! The only change was the sheets were stowed away, but the political goals, willingness, and capability to follow through on them carried on. They are still at it they never went away. Dr. Fleming states that 'General Albert Pike, who stood high in the Masonic order, was the chief judicial officer of the Klan'. Albert Pike also wrote extensively on the mythical super-race of the Aryans, extolling their virtues, imagined history, and religion, which he tried to show, was the precursor of Freemasonry in his numerous Published Works. It would seem that Pike was a fellow traveler with Blavatsky on this subject. Fifty years later in Central Europe there will be others who will take up this mantle and use these writings as the basis for an ideology that curiously enough, will also use the term 'new world order' to describe their agenda, Just a co-incidence of course.

The Asiatic Nations comprise eleven twelfths of the world's population, and the European Nations, one twelfth; the Asiatic Nations and the Roman Cross Order of Christ and Mary in the US are under the Magna Carta but do not know this. The Magna Carta of 1854 Philadelphia, the chief city of Pennsylvania, founded by William Penn and other Quakers helped in the granting of freedom to the blond masses.

The Europeans who have agreed by oath, or secret obligation to protect their society and prevent the legal marriage or socialization with people of heavy olive shade of skin, referred to as Asiatic or Original. Should any of these men and women violate the code, they are subject to become a social outcast of their society, especially if the violation involves marriage to any of the Asiatic men and/or women. This is a major violation of the Clannish society of the pale skin world, although the grown sons of the Klan society are at liberty to shop around with the Asiatic women of the US. The US Constitution is a document that granted economic, social and commercial freedom and equality to all people of ruddy pale skin, regardless to label and religious or political faith.

Eugene Tallmadge was a major figure in Georgia politics from 1933 thru 1945; he opposed President Franklin D. Roosevelt's administration to establish its New Deal programs of economic relief in the states. Tallmadge was born in 1884 and died in 1946. He ran for the U.S. Senate in 1936 and 1938, losing in both bids. As a member of the Board of Regents, which oversees public higher education in Georgia, Tallmadge used this to have a professor fired for having 'integrationist' views, The University eventually lost its accreditation, and Tallmadge was defeated for reelection in 1942.

Theodore Gilmore Bilbo, Democratic Senator from Mississippi, Bilbo was a Governor in 1928, he advocated the deportation of Moors to Africa, and he called Congresswoman Claire Booth Luce a nigger lover and in 1938 praised Adolph Hitler on the floor of the Senate.

He attacked miscegenation stating that one drop of Negro blood placed in the veins of a Caucasian woman destroys the inventive genius of the European-American's mind. Bilbo was born October 13, 1877, and was the 32nd Governor of Mississippi.

A Senate committee found him guilty of accepting bribes from military contractors during WWII and he was denied his seat in the Senate in 1947, he died in New Orleans on August 21, 1947.

The insignia on the US dime of 1865 represents the staff of the Roman Ax, which unfortunately left the Moors or Asiatic descendants on the outside looking in during the past 142 years of Roman economic social and commercial stride. Father Abraham, the god of the Roman Union involving the North and South or January 1 and July 4.

Abraham Lincoln

Take all of the US Coins and line them up together heads up, what do you see? (Look at Abraham's head verse the other President's heads)

Abraham Lincoln was said to be the illegitimate son of a Moor. In his campaign for the Presidency he was referred to as a Black-a-Moor by his opponents, he was even depicted as a Moor; he was called 'Abraham-Africanus the First'. (The Hidden Lincoln 1938)

If you are cynical, you can go to the library and ask for the history of the Asiatic Empire, and carefully observe the European Americans reactions. Then you should denounce the names, Negro, Colored, Black Afro-American and African American. In this book, is the history; the European American has thought you would never read, nevertheless, you have the fundamentals in your heart just listen.

Empires

During the 1,411 years that have past there have been only two world empires, The Asiatic Empire of The Order of Islam and The Roman Empire of The Order of Christ and Mary. The era of the US Order of Christ is 217 years old, calculated from 1774, the era that resulted in the birth of the US Marine Force in colonial North America the cream of the English, Francisco, and Germans also the French Legions, Spanish Armada and the Pirates. Not to be confused with The Order of Christianity 551 years old calculated from 1932, the year of the Peasants Revolt also called Tyler's Rebellion, against Richard II as in the poll tax in June 1381.

Moreover, let us not forget the preacher John Ball a priest in Kent who was an opponent of feudalism, and preached the doctrines of the English theologian and religious reformer John Wycliffe and advocated social equality. John Ball was executed at Saint Albans in the presence of King Richard II of England.

John Wycliffe was a theologian, which attracted the support and patronage of royalty because he developed ideas that supported increased power of the monarchy over the church and the clergy. His ideas helped to incite the Peasants Revolt of 1381.

He preached in English and wrote some English tracts, but no English writings of his survived. There are 36 manuscripts inspired by him, yet he did not contribute to the translation of the bible into English.

Like the Waldensians, the Lollards translated the Bible into their vernacular language, English. The Lollards were the most significant heretical group in England before popes Gregory XI and Urban VI condemned the Reformation of Wycliffe on several occasions. Even after his death, Wycliffe's heretical teachings were addressed at the Council of Constance in 1415.

Followers of Wycliffe came to be known as Lollards, the sect was driven out of Oxford in 1382, but some devout members circulated Wycliffe's teachings as well as the 1,394 Lollards Conclusions. John Wycliffe was both a great champion of the Reformation and a failure. Though his reforms did begin to take hold, they were put down within his lifetime. Not until Martin Luther nailed his theses to the door at Wittenberg did the seeds of Wycliffe's legacy bloom into the Reformation. **(See Ch 19 of this book)**

The Continental Congress authorized the formation of two battalions of US Marines on November 10, 1775, to fight in the American Revolution 1775 thru 1783. The first Marine landing occurred when a force of Marines captured New Province Island in the Bahamas from the British on March 3 1776.

Marines served on both land and sea during the remainder of the Revolutionary War, were deactivated after the war ended, as was the Continental Navy in 1783. John Hanson a member of Congress from the state of Maryland had a legal battle started in the United States Congress in 1778 ending in 1781. The fight was over the distribution of the land known at the time as the North West Country. This land had been taken by England and was later known as Ohio, Indiana, Michigan, Wisconsin and Illinois.

John Hanson took the floor of Congress and protested against the demands of the 12 States. He told them that no state had any rights to any land, and that NJ, NY or any other state did not win the war. He said that the united efforts of all the states on the battlefields won the war; therefore, all the land belonged to all the people under the Federal Government, the United States of America.

Hanson kept fighting until he finally subdued the 12 rebellious states and drove them back into the Union, he also compelled them to sign back any claims they had in land to the US or Federal Union. When the 12 signed, Maryland signed right after as the 13th state March 1, 1781. During the Asiatic world domination, there was not any Europe, England, France, Greece, Rome, Egypt, Africa, or Russia across the Atlantic and the Pacific Ocean. Therefore, US history of the Christian Order might be compared with that of the celebrated story referred to as Santa Claus. (Mythology) Did you ever stop to think that on the most sacred day of the Christian Order (December 25th), the Christian Nations promulgates the world's greatest false-hood, the myth of Santa Claus. Remember, December 25th is the foundation of the philosophy of Christ and Mary.

Now you can draw your own conclusion upon the European image strange Son of God, who lend deaf ears to hear your plea or prayer.

Nations without a flag to represent them are dead nation; that is to say, their names are not written in the universal book of law.

Black people, Brown people, Red people, African American, Negroes, Coloreds and Indians do not have a flag to represent them because these people do not exist. The entire world of people comprises only Asiatics, amalgamated Asiatics, and Europeans. The 5 and 7 point Star, the Crescent the Cedar tree is the insignia of the Asiatic or Asiatic Nation, and it is the Mother of all National Banners of the world today. The Asiatic Flag represents the entire Asiatic family some four billion four hundred million, upon this ball of matter, termed Earth. It gave birth to the banner of the Iron Cross Legions, or the German tribes of Europe all the way to South America.

The French banner and the banner of the stars and stripes, the banner with the double cross or eight points which represent the British caste, the house of Lords of the Roman World spring from this. With all power, political and commercial openly and secretly directed from the US. (E pluribus Unum) On US money is a Latin phrase, which implies one out of many, One Nation of many races and sub-nations of the Roman Cross Order.

War
William the Conqueror
September 28, 1066

Claiming his right to the English throne, William, the Duke of Normandy, invades England on Britain's southeast coast. His subsequent defeat of King Harold II at the Battle of Hastings marked the beginning of a new era in British history. William was the illegitimate son of Robert I, the Duke of Normandy, by his concubine Arleta. The Duke, who had no other sons, designated William his heir, and with his death in 1035, William became the Duke of Normandy at age seven. Rebellions were epidemic during the early years of his reign, and on several occasions, the young Duke narrowly escaped death. Many of his advisers did not, when he was 20, William had become an able ruler of whom King Henry I of France backed. Henry later turned against him, but William survived the opposition and in 1063 expanded his borders into the region of Maine. In 1051, William visited England and met with his cousin Edward the Confessor, the childless English King, according to Norman historians, Edward promised to make William his heir, on his deathbed, however, Edward granted the Kingdom to Harold Godwine, head of the leading Noble family in England who was more powerful than Edward the King was. In January 1066, King Edward died, and Harold Godwine was proclaimed King Harold II. William immediately disputed his claim.

In addition, King Harold III (Hardraade of Norway) had designs on England, as did Tostig; Tostig was born the third son of Godwin, Earl of Wessex and Kent, and Gytha Thorkelsdóttir. In 1051, he married Judith, the daughter of Count Baldwin IV his half-sister of Baldwin the brother of Harold.

King Harold rallied his forces for an expected invasion by William, but Tostig launched a series of raids instead, forcing the King to leave the English Channel unprotected. In September, Tostig joined forces with King Harold III and invaded England from Scotland. On September 25, Harold met them at the Stamford Bridge, defeated, and killed them both. Three days later, William landed in England at Pevensey. With approximately 7,000 troops and cavalry, William seized Pevensey and marched to Hastings, where he paused to organize his forces. On October 13, Harold arrived near Hastings with his army, and the next day William led his forces out to give battle. At the end of a bloody, all-day battle, King Harold II was killed shot in the eye with an arrow, according to legend and his forces were defeated. William then marched on London and received the city's submission. On Christmas Day, 1066, William the Conqueror crowned the first Norman king of England, in Westminster Abbey, and the Anglo-Saxon phase of English history ended.

French became the language of the King's Court and gradually blended with the Anglo-Saxon tongue to give birth to modern English. William I proved an effective King of England, and the Domes-day Book, a great census of the lands and people of England, was among his notable achievements. Upon the death of William I in 1087, his son, William Rufus, became William II, the second Norman king of England. British and American representatives at Belgium, ending the War of 1812, sign the Treaty of Peace and Amity between His Britannic Majesty and the US, by the terms of the treaty, all conquered territory was to be returned, and commissions were planned to settle the boundary of the US and Canada. In June 1812, the US declared war against Great Britain in reaction to three issues: the British economic blockade of France, the induction of thousands of neutral American seamen into the British Royal Navy against their will, and the British support of so-called Indian tribes along the Great Lakes frontier.

A faction of Congress, made up mostly of western and southern congressional representatives, had been advocating the declaration of war for several years. These 'War Hawks', as they were known, hoped that war with Britain, which was preoccupied with its struggle against Napoleonic France, would result in US territorial gains in Canada and British protected Florida. In the months following the US declaration of war, American forces launched a three-point invasion of Canada, all of which were repulsed. At sea, however, the US was more successful, and the USS Constitution and other American frigates won a series of victories over British warships. In 1813, American forces won several key victories in the Great Lakes region, but Britain regained control of the sea and blockaded the eastern seaboard. In 1814, with the downfall of Napoleon, the British were able to allocate greater amount of military resources to the American war, and Washington, D.C., fell to the British in August. In Washington, British troops burned the White House, the Capitol, and other buildings in retaliation for the earlier burning of government buildings in Canada by US soldiers. Fort McHenry in Baltimore harbor withstood a massive British bombardment, on September 11, 1814, the tide of the war turned when the American naval force won a decisive victory at the Battle of Plattsburg Bay on Lake Champlain, a large British army is forced to abandon its invasion of the US (To the northeast side) and retreated to Canada.

The American victory on Lake Champlain led to the conclusion of US and British peace negotiations in Belgium, and on December 24, 1814, the Treaty of Ghent is signed, ending the war. News of the treaty took almost two months to cross the Atlantic, and British forces were not informed of the end of hostilities in time to end their drive against the mouth of the Mississippi River. On January 8, 1815, the 'British army attacked New Orleans and is decimated by the American forces', under General Andrew Jackson. The American public heard of the Battle of New Orleans and the Treaty of Ghent at approximately the same time, fostering a greater sentiment of self-confidence and shared identity throughout the 'young republic for the European'.

SLAVERY ABOLISHED IN AMERICA
December 18, 1865
Chapter 8

Following its ratification by the requisite three-quarters of the states earlier in the month, the 13th Amendment is adopted into the US Constitution ensuring that neither slavery nor involuntary servitude shall exist within the US nor any place subject to their jurisdiction. Before the American Civil War, Abraham Lincoln and other leaders of the anti-slavery Republican Party sought not to abolish slavery but merely to stop its extension into new territories and states in the American West.

This policy was unacceptable to most Southern politicians, who believed that the growth of Free states would turn the US power structure irrevocably against them. In November 1860, Lincoln's election as President signaled the secession of seven southern states and the formation of the Confederate states of America. Shortly after his inauguration in 1861, the Civil War began. Four more states that are southern joined the Confederacy, while four border slave states in the upper south remained in the Union. Lincoln, though he privately detested slavery, responded cautiously to the call by abolitionists for emancipation of all American slaves.

However as the war dragged on, the Republican-dominated federal government began to realize the strategic advantages of emancipation: The liberation of slaves would weaken the Confederacy by depriving it of a major portion of its labor force, which would in turn strengthen the Union by producing an influx of workers. When 11 southern states seceded from the Union, there were few pro-slavery congressional representatives to stand in the way of such an action. In 1862, Congress annulled the fugitive slave laws, prohibited slavery in the US territories, and authorized Lincoln to employ freed slaves in the army.

Following a major Union victory in September, Lincoln issued a warning of his intent to issue an emancipation proclamation for all states still in rebellion on New Year's Day. That day January 1, 1863, President Lincoln formally issued the Emancipation Proclamation, 'calling on the Union army to liberate all slaves in states still in rebellion as an act of justice, warranted by the Constitution, upon military necessity'. These three million slaves are declared to be 'then, thenceforward, and forever free'.

The proclamation exempted the border slave states that remained in the Union and all or parts of three Confederate states controlled by the Union Army. The Emancipation Proclamation transformed the Civil War from a war against secession into a war for 'a new birth of freedom', as Lincoln stated in his Gettysburg Address in 1863. This ideological change discouraged the intervention of France and England on the Confederacy's behalf and enabled the Union to enlist the 180,000 African American soldiers and sailors who volunteered to fight between January 1, 1863, and the conclusion of the war. As the Confederacy staggered toward defeat, Lincoln realized that the Emancipation Proclamation, a war measure, might have little constitutional authority once the war was over. The Republican Party subsequently introduced the 13th Amendment into Congress, and in April 1864, the necessary two-thirds of the overwhelmingly Republican Senate passed the amendment. However, the House of Representatives, featuring a higher proportion of Democrats, did not pass the amendment by a two-thirds majority until January 1865, three months before Confederate General Robert E. Lee surrender at Appomattox.

On December 2, 1865, Alabama became the 27th state to ratify the 13th Amendment, thus giving it the requisite three-fourths majority of state approval necessary to make it the law of the land. Alabama, a former Confederate state, was forced to ratify the amendment as a condition for re-admission into the Union. On December 18, the 13th Amendment was officially adopted into the Constitution 246 years after the first shipload of captive Africans landed at Jamestown, Virginia, and were known among themselves as POW. Slavery and her legacy with the efforts to overcome it remained a central issue in US politics for more than a century, particularly during the post-Civil War Reconstruction era and the African American civil rights movement of the 1950 thru 1960.

Much of America's understanding of the early relationship between the Indian and the European is conveyed through the story of Thanksgiving. Proclaimed a holiday in 1863 by Abraham Lincoln, this fairy tale of a feast was allowed to exist in the American imagination untouched until 1970, the 350th anniversary of the landing of the Pilgrims. That is when Frank B. James, (president of the Federated Eastern Indian League), prepared a speech for a Plymouth banquet that exposed the Pilgrims for having committed, the robbery of the graves of the Wampanoag's. He wrote we welcomed you, the white man, with open arms, little knowing that it was the beginning of the end of life as he new it; that before 50 years were to pass, the Wampanoag would no longer be a free people.

However, European Massachusetts officials told him he could not deliver such a speech and offered to write him another. Instead, James declined to speak, and on Thanksgiving Day, hundreds of Native Americans from around the country came to protest.
It was the first National Day of Mourning, a day to mark the losses Native Americans suffered as the early settlers prospered.

Thanksgiving

This true story of 'Thanksgiving' is what Europeans did not want Mr. James to tell, what really happened in Plymouth in 1621? According to a single paragraph account in the writings of one Pilgrim, a harvest feast did take place in Plymouth in 1621, probably in October, but the Native Americans who attended were not even invited. Though it later became known as Thanksgiving, the Pilgrims never called it that. In addition, amidst the imagery of a picnic of interracial harmony is some of the most terrifying bloodshed in New World history.

The Pilgrim crop had failed miserably that year, but the agricultural expertise of the Native Americans had produced twenty acres of corn, without which the Pilgrims would have surely perished. The so-called Indians often brought food to the Pilgrims, who came from England ridiculously unprepared to survive and hence relied almost exclusively on handouts from the overly generous Native Americans thus making the Pilgrims the western hemisphere's first class of welfare recipients.

The Pilgrims invited the Native American Sachem Massasoit to their feast, and it was Massasoit, engaging in the tribal tradition of equal sharing, who then invited ninety or more of his brothers and sisters to the annoyance of the 50 or so ungrateful Europeans. No turkey, cranberry sauce or pumpkin pie was served; they ate duck, geese and venison from the five deer brought by Massasoit. In fact, all, of the food was brought and prepared by the Native Americans, whose 10,000 years of familiarity with the cuisine of the region had kept the Europeans alive up to that point. The Pilgrims wore no black hats or buckled shoes these were the silly inventions of artists hundreds of years since that time.

These lower-class Englishmen wore brightly colored clothing, with one of their church leaders recording among his possessions one pair of green drawers. Contrary to the fabricated lore of storyteller's generations since, no Pilgrims prayed at the meal, and the supposed good cheer and fellowship must have dissipated quickly once the Pilgrims brandished their weaponry in a primitive display of intimidation. The Pilgrims consumed a good deal of home brew. In fact, each Pilgrim drank at least a half gallon of beer a day, which they preferred even to water. This daily inebriation led their governor, William Bradford, to comment on his people's 'notorious sin', which included their 'drunkenness and unseemliness' and rampant sodomy. The Pilgrims of Plymouth, the Original Scalpers Contrary to popular mythology, were no friends to the local Native Americans. They were engaged in a ruthless war of extermination against their hosts, even as they falsely posed as friends. Just days before the alleged Thanksgiving love fest, a company of Pilgrims led by Myles Standish actively sought to chop off the head of a local chief. They deliberately caused a rivalry between two friendly Native Americans, pitting one against the other in an attempt to obtain better intelligence and make them both more diligent. An 11-foot-high wall was erected around the entire settlement for keeping the Native Americans out. Any so-called Indian who came within the vicinity of the Pilgrim settlement was subject to robbery, enslavement, or even murder.

The Pilgrims further advertised their evil intentions and racial hostility, when they mounted five cannons on a hill around their settlement, constructed a platform for artillery, and then organized their soldiers into four companies all in preparation for the military destruction of their friends the so-called Indians. Pilgrim Myles Standish eventually got his bloody prize. He went to the Native Americans, pretended to be a trader, and then beheaded a Native American man named Wituwamat. He brought the head to Plymouth, where it was displayed on a wooden spike for many years, according to Gary B. Nash, as a symbol of European power. Standish had the so-called Indian man's young brother hanged from the rafters for good measure. From that time on, the Europeans were known to the Native Americans of Massachusetts by the name Wotowquenange, which in their tongue meant cutthroats and stabbers. The myth of the fierce, ruthless so-called Indian savage lusting after the blood of innocent Europeans must be vigorously dispelled at this point. In actuality, the historical record shows that the very opposite was true. Once the European settlements stabilized, the Europeans turned on their hosts in a brutal way. The once amicable relationship was breeched repeatedly by the Europeans, who lusted over the riches of so-called Indian lands. A combination of the Pilgrims' demonization of the so-called Indians, the concocted mythology of Eurocentric historians, and standard Hollywood propaganda has served to paint the gentle Native Americans as a tomahawk-swinging savage endlessly on the warpath, lusting for the blood of the God-fearing Europeans.

However, the Pilgrims' own testimony obliterates that fallacy. The so-called Indians engaged each other in military contests from time to time, but the causes of war, the methods, and the resulting damage differed profoundly from the European variety: The Indian wars were largely symbolic and were about honor, not about territory or extermination. The Wars were fought as domestic correction for a specific act and were ended when correction was achieved. Such action might better be described as internal policing. The conquest or destruction of whole territories was a European concept. The Indian wars were often engaged in by family groups, not by tribal groups, and would involve only the family members. The lengthy negotiation was engaged in between the aggrieved parties before escalation to physical confrontation would be sanctioned. Surprise attacks were unknown to the Indians. It was regarded as evidence of bravery for a man to go into battle carrying no weapon that would do any harm at a distance not even bows and arrows. The bravest act in war in some Native American cultures was to touch their adversary and escape before he could do physical harm. The targeting of non-combatants like women, children, and the elderly was never contemplated. Native Americans expressed shock and repugnance when the Europeans told, and then showed, them that they considered women and children fair game in their style of warfare.

The major Native American wars might end with less than a dozen casualties on both sides. Often, when the arrows had been expended the war would be halted. The European practice of wiping out whole nations in bloody massacres was incomprehensible to the Indian. According to one scholar, the most notable feature of Native American warfare was its relative innocuity. European observers of Native American war often expressed surprise at how little harm they actually inflicted. Their wars are far less bloody and devouring than the cruel wars of Europe, commented settler Roger Williams in 1643.

Even Puritan warmonger and professional soldier Capt. John Mason scoffed at so-called Indian warfare: Their feeble manner did hardly deserve the name of fighting. Fellow warmonger John Underhill spoke of the Narragansetts, after having spent a day burning and spoiling their country: no Indians would come near us, but run from us, as the deer from the dogs. He concluded that the so-called Indians might fight seven years and not kill seven men. Their fighting style, he wrote, is more for pastime, than to conquer and subdue enemies. All this describes a people for whom war is a deeply regrettable last resort. An agrarian people, the Native Americans had devised a civilization that provided dozens of options all designed to avoid conflict the very opposite of Europeans, for whom all out war, a ferocious bloodlust, and systematic genocide are their apparent life force. Thomas Jefferson who himself advocated the physical extermination of the American so-called Indian said of Europe, They [The Europeans] are nations of eternal war. All their energies are expended in the destruction of labor, property and lives of their people. (See the Puritan Holocaust) By 1630, a new group of 700 'even holier' Europeans calling themselves Puritans had arrived on 11 ships and settled in Boston which only served to accelerate the brutality against the so-called Indians. In one incident around 1637, a force of Europeans trapped some seven hundred Pequot, mostly women, children, and the elderly, near the mouth of the Mystic River. Englishman John Mason attacked the camp with fire, sword, blunderbuss, and tomahawk. Only a handful escaped and few prisoners were taken to the apparent delight of the Europeans: To see them frying in the fire, and the streams of their blood quenching the same, and the stench was horrible; but the victory seemed a sweet sacrifice, and they gave praise thereof to God. This event marked the first actual Thanksgiving. In just 10 years, 12,000 Europeans had invaded New England, and as their numbers grew, they pressed for all out extermination of the Native Americans. Euro-diseases had reduced the population of the Massachusetts nation from over 24,000 to less than 750; meanwhile, the number of European settlers in Massachusetts rose to more than 20,000 by 1646. By 1675, the Massachusetts Englishmen were in a full-scale war with the great chief of the Wampanoag's, Metacomet. Renamed 'King Philip' by the European, Metacomet watched the steady erosion of the lifestyle, culture of his people as Europeans imposed laws, and values engulfed them. In 1671, the European had ordered Metacomet to come to Plymouth to enforce upon him a new treaty, which included the humiliating rule that he could no longer sell his own land without prior approval from Europeans. They also demanded that he turn in his community's firearms. Marked for extermination by the merciless power of a distant king and his ruthless subjects, Metacomet retaliated in 1675 with raids on several isolated frontier towns. Eventually, they attacked 52 of the 90 New England towns, destroying 13 of them. The Englishmen ultimately regrouped, and after much bloodletting defeated the great Nation, just half a century after their arrival on Massachusetts soil.

Historian Douglas Edward Leach describes the end, 'The ruthless executions, the cruel sentences, were all aimed at the same goal the unchallengeable European supremacy in southern New England. That the program succeeded is convincingly demonstrated by the almost complete docility of the local native ever since. When Captain Benjamin Church tracked down and murdered Metacomet in 1676, his body was quartered and parts were left for the wolves.

The great Indian chief's hands were cut off and sent to Boston and his head went to Plymouth, where it was set upon a pole on the real first day of public Thanksgiving for the beginning of revenge upon the enemy'. Metacomet's nine-year-old son was destined for execution because, the Europeans reasoned, the 'offspring of the devil must pay for the sins of their father'. The child was instead shipped to the Caribbean to spend his life in slavery. As the Holocaust continued, several official Thanksgiving Days were proclaimed. Governor Joseph Dudley declared in 1704 a 'General Thanksgiving' not in celebration of fellowship of man but for God's infinite Goodness to extend His Favors. In defeating and disappointing, the Expeditions of the Enemy [so-called Indians] against us, And the good Success given us against them, by delivering so many of them into our hands, Just two years later one could reap a hefty reward in Massachusetts for the scalp of a so-called Indian demonstrating that the practice of scalping was a European tradition. According to one scholar, 'Hunting redskins became a popular sport in New England, especially since so-called Indian prisoners were worth good money'.

ASIATIC OR BLACK LANGUAGES
Chapter 9

Prior to 1828, the Roman tribes of colonial North America were speaking various dialects of Latin. The first English dictionary was published in colonial North America in 1828. Thus, the English Language is the manifestation of all dialects, which were derived from Arabic and Hebrew, which is derived from classical Aramaic. All came from the same foundation as Arabic, you will also see in this order, Ancient Hebrew, Phoenicia, Southern Arabic and the Hieroglyph or 'Medu-Neters' words of the Gods or Divine writings all came from the original man. The French, Spanish and Italian employ practically the same expressions in language, the German and Jew employ the very same expression in language, and this tangible evidence has fully explained the E-Pluribus-Unum on US money, 'one out of many'.

History of the Asiatic Black Nation

The history of the Asiatic Nation lies hidden in the library of every State of the Union, and also in the library of practically every home if you know were to look. Therefore, the history of the Asiatic Nation is not news but a guide to the true history of the world. The European American hid the truth from the so-called Negro under the influence of fear and hatred starting in the year of 1555 AD.

Prophet Muhummed and the split of Arabia

The Prophet Muhummed was born in Mecca in the year 570 years after the Christian era, in the year 610 ace; Muhammad receives the revelations from Allah through the Angle Gabriel. In the year 622 AD, the Flight (Hegira) took place; Prophet Muhummed flees Mecca and finds refuge in Yathrib. This is day one in the Muslim calendar. Around 630 thru 631 AD, the Unification of the Arabian Peninsula had taken place. In the year 632 AD, the Prophet Muhummed left his physical body.

In the years 635 thru 650 AD, Under the Caliphs, Conquest of Syria, Palestine, the Persian Empire, Egypt and parts of North Africa, West Africa and Spain was accomplished. Six hundred and thirty eight AD was the year that the Muslims captured Jerusalem. 650 AD, Abu Bakr and Umar establish the final writings of the Qur'an.

Uthman is accused, of favoring his relatives when making important and sometimes lucrative appointments, of diverting monies from the treasury, and of other transgressions, some fiscal, and some moral. This dissension grew into a violent uprising, which culminated in the murder of the caliph in 656 AD. These developments began the complicated series of events known as the First Civil War (656 – 661), which was a struggle for leadership of the community of believers waged by the prominent heads of several families within the Prophet's tribe, the 'Quraysh'. This is of utmost importance in Islamic history, because this is when the main subgroups or 'sects' that have constituted the Muslim community up to the present day first emerged.

The first Civil War finally ended in 661 AD, when Kharijite assassin killed Ali. In 650 thru 732 AD, is the Muslim Expansion into Eastern Turkey, India and China. In 673 thru 797 AD, there were repeated attempts to penetrate deeper into Europe and capture Constantinople, the capital of the Greek Byzantine Empire. Leo IV defeats the famous Muslim swordsmen twice, and then dies of Anthrax in 780 AD at the age of 30. In the year 1453 AD, 'The Collapse of the Byzantine Empire takes place when the Ottoman Turks finally captured Constantinople'.

Asiatics & Moors Are the Same People (Black, Brown, Red & Yellow)

It is impossible for the people of heavy ripe olive shade of skin to become a Christian because of this fact. The Christians worship a European son of God and his mother Mary, the very image of themselves; the Christian God is European because his only begotten son is tangible evidence of this fact. You might ask yourself this question, what chance do I have to enter the gates of the Christian Heaven dominated by a European God, his son and his son's mother Mary? The very image of the woman who falsely cries rape followed by her sons with their cross burning, and their lynching of the Black Man.

On the contrary there is a specific reason for the new masses of humanity referred to as Europeans to establish the church and the doctrine of Christ and Mary, so let us observe this in order that we might take a broad view that will enable us to erase the hatred against them which is now dominating our world.

It has already been stated that during the past 1,411 years there has only been two world Empires, The Asiatic Empires of the Order of Islam and the Christian Empire of the Order of Christ. The Presbyterian professed the 'true Christ', the Methodist professed the 'true Christ', the Mormon professed the 'true Christ', the Roman Catholics also professed the 'true Christ', and all of them denounced all others as false. This system at one time prohibited the issuance of a marriage license to Asiatic men and woman, who desire to marry European men and women in North America especially in the United States of America.

Jehovah Witness

The Jehovah Witness and the World Wide Church of God, the Plane Truth Organization of today endeavoring to up-lift the Orders of Christ. Remember the founders and heads of these organizations are the same people, also referred to as Europeans, therefore, we might say that the organization of the Jehovah Witness and the World Wide Church of God will wake up the European masses?

Roman Republican Party 138 Years Ago

In the year 1854, the European women often referred to as The Daughters of the American Revolution endorse the artistic painting of themselves and son, called Christ and Mary, by force, intrigue ignorance, cruelty, seduction, bloodshed and destruction. The foundation of the Order of Christ was well laid in the Union of 1865. This was followed by well-trained Missionary workers carrying the banner of the image son and Mother Doctrine across the Pacific and Atlantic Oceans, supported by military force of the Order of Rome. Thereby, the false doctrine of the pale Son Christ was established in the four angles of the Earth. This enabled the pale skin Daughters of the Revolution to remain neutral, while the pale skin men seduced the helpless Asiatic or Asiatic women at home and abroad, to perpetuate the pale skin Nation of Rome during the past 138 years.

The picture of the son image and Mother equal the power of ten thousand words in the name of the tradition of European-American superiority. When placed before the blond children, raging between six and nine years of age, this gave them a false conception of European supremacy before they can read, and this is how they grow up to be men and women the world over. The 138-year-old act of the Daughters of the American Revolution has disqualified the English women at home and abroad yet they play their specific roll in the New World Order, which is now rapidly progressing. Actually, the English-speaking women have disqualified all other European women of different languages from playing in the New World Order. Today it is the pale women's desire to tell the truth and alter the Roman system of segregation but 85% of the Asiatic masses of the world will not believe in them, owing to the long brain washing of the world to the on going trend of economic and social suffering. This part of the story is referred to as a view of the promise land, but you cannot enter.

Generations of Blond Sons and Subjugated Asiatic Women

Had not the Muslims of Saudi Arabia established the superstitious religious system contrary to the universal economic and social science as shown in the Qur'an, twelve signs of the zodiac and ten numbers of mathematics, there would have been no superstitious religious Orders of today. Therefore, the fact is that both, Muslims, Christians and Jews of the entire earth are equally guilty for violation of the Law of Nature as shown in the twelve signs of the ever present zodiac which has cause them to undergo the Law of retribution.

The Asiatic Nation submitted to the law of retribution in 1555, 1774, and 1776. The Roman Cross Nations submitted to the law of retribution in 1914, to be fulfilled in 15,084 of the Asiatic calendar. This will culminate a short cycle of 84 years. 15,084 mark the end of the doctrine of the Daughters of the American Revolution, the Church mystery system, race and color.

Civilization is founded upon practical knowledge, wisdom, understanding and the morals of women. The Asiatic (Black) women have undergone everything that could have been imposed upon them, yet they retained their morals. You may compare the acts of the lamb's wool hair woman of the US and abroad with the acts of the European blond woman of the US and abroad and thereby draw your own conclusion during the next 170 years of global economic and social revolution. Thousands of blond women and sons will resort to suicide while undergoing the 170 years of economic and social revolution.

The lambs' wool of the so-called Black-men in North America and abroad will restore civilization and peace to the world during the next 170 years, Geometry and the twelve signs of the Zodiac constitute the Prophetic law, which has never told a lie. The economic suffering of the blond women of Rome, England, France, Germany and Greece and the mythical Palestine will be fulfill with the blond women of the US, Canada and Australia during the next 170 years. Nature has a just law, the law of retribution that cannot be off set with a dream, lip service, hypocritical prayer, wealth, atomic bombs, military training and the wooden or stone image European God. The economic chaos of the FDIC will make the blond people of the US, hate the names such as; Black, Brown, Red and Yellow and love the name Asiatic.

After the cycle of retribution has been fulfilled by the Asiatics of the United States, the Daughters of the American Revolution will end-up begging the Asiatics who have given birth to children who have become champions of the world in every important department of society. Remember champions of the world do not have to beg for social recognition. The law of retribution cannot be altered. We reap that which has been sown in the past.

The Greek, Jew and Latin of the Roman Cross Order definitely cannot go beyond the Moabite Alphabet. Our Asiatic ancestors' codes of Alphabet and Mathematics have proven that the pale person has no culture of his own.

The Asiatic shade code in electronics, which describes the unit of resistance, current and voltage, the magnetic law, atomic energy is as follows, blue, red, green, orange, yellow, brown, violet, gray, white and black. The Asiatic fore fathers had harnessed atomic energy and employed it for both good and ill many centuries before the European red-skinned blond-haired women of Patagonia had become educated by the cultured Moors. Atomic energy is new to the pale person, but not to the Asiatic Nation. The Christians race and color scheme was founded upon the Asiatic color code of electronics. It is impossible for a nation that is dominated by various secret orders that are to hold the Asiatic man and woman back to solve its economic and social problems.

You might ask your self this question. How can one help him self and others without exposing his secrets?

The code of mathematics from knowledge to born and born back to knowledge

(- 12 9 6 3 0 3 6 9 12 +) constitutes the ever present code of law which never grows old or Ancient. Neither Earth, Water, Air and Heat Light or Electricity will ever grow old or ancient, the whole of which comprise the one great body of the ever-present living truth that there is no mystery god and neither a secret.

All secret orders involving religion, symbolism and mystic passwords are our own signs of ignorance of the realities that dwell within us and about us. That which individuals have in their minds unexpressed is a secret. Having expressed it then the great secret has been exposed to the outer world.

The inner world of the mind, must not be confined to the physical or three-dimensional plane, but including every plane and every type of life form, through which mind or soul expresses it-self. This excludes the findings of European psychology, which confines its attention to the physical world. Inner processes are largely recognized by their external effects. There are not two minds. What is called objective consciousness or objective Mind, which there is a growing tendency upon the part of some psychologists to call clear consciousness is merely a portion of the Mind-Soul or Unconscious-Mind as you choose to term it manifesting through the physical brain. To do this it utilizes electric energies to impart vibratory rates to the brain cells. Thus, our Unconscious-Mind is the inner world referred to as the All Seeing Eye.

In our physical universe positive and negative charges of electricity as protons and electrons are the building blocks of which all the elements of matter are composed. In a similar manner, all true thought elements are composed of Reproductive Desires and Nutritive Desires in some proportion. That is, the elements belonging to ten distinct families of which the psycho plasma in the thought cells is composed, they called this reproductive desires and nutritive desires. Thus, woman is the grand master architecture and carpenter of the physical body. This makes all equality or things that take up space Muslims due the fact that they all submit to the will of the Creator.

Babies are nine months from conception to birth, the number nine has many names one is Nimrod. The Christmas tree is an evergreen tree, and has life all year round. *Santa Clause* robbing Asiatic people at Christmas is similar to Nimrod's work. **December 25th** is the birthday of Nimrod; Nimrod killed his father and married his mother whose name was Ester, today called Easter. When Nimrod's wife (mother) had her first child he feared that the people would lose respect for him if they knew he was making babies through his own mother (it was a secret that they were married) therefore to fool the people Nimrod told the people that the Holy Ghost had impregnated his mother. This was the beginning of the great lie told about the birth of Jesus and his Mother Mary.

SON OF MAN
Chapter 10

On September 24, 622 AD, the Prophet Muhammad completes his Hegira, or "flight," from Mecca to Medina to escape persecution. In Medina, Muhammad set about building the followers of his creed Islam into an organized community. The Hegira would later mark the beginning (year 1) of the Muslim calendar. Muhammad, the Prophet is one of the most influential religious and political leaders in history, born in Mecca around 570. His father died before he was born, and Muhammad was put under the care of his grandfather, head of the prestigious Hashim clan. His mother died when he was six, and his grandfather when he was eight, leaving him under the care of his uncle Abu Talib, the new head of the clan. When he was 25, Muhammad married a wealthy widow 15 years his senior. He lived the next 15 years as a merchant, and his wife gave birth to six children: two sons, (who died in childhood), and four daughters.

Elijah Muhummed

Elijah Muhammad was born on or about Oct. 7, 1897 in Sandersville, Georgia. Elijah Poole married Clara Evans, of Georgia. They had eight children, Emmanuel, Ethel, Lottie, Nathaniel, Herbert, Elijah, Jr., Wallace and Akbar. In April 1923, Elijah Poole moved his young family from Macon, Georgia, where he worked for the Southern Railroad Company and the Cherokee Brick Company to Detroit, Mich. Detroit was a bustling upwardly mobile city with a booming auto industry. On July 4, 1930, the long awaited 'Savior' of the so-called Black man and woman, Master Fard Muhammad, appeared in the city. He announced and preached that God is one, and it is now time for Blacks to return to the Religion of their Ancestors, Islam. News spread all over the city of Detroit of the preaching of this great man from the East. Elijah Poole's wife first learned of the Temple of Islam and wanted to attend to see what the commotion was all about, but instead, her husband advised her that he would go and see for himself. In 1931, while preaching WD Fard met Elijah Poole, He asked him to be His Divine Representative in continuing this most difficult task of bringing truth and light to His lost and found people. For 3 1/2 years, He taught and trained Elijah Muhammad night and day into the profound Secret Wisdom of the Reality of God. This included the hidden knowledge of the original people who were the first founders of civilization of our Planet and who had a full knowledge of the Universal Order of Things from the beginning of the Divine Creation. Upon the Master's departure in 1934, Elijah Muhammad labored tirelessly to bring life to his mentally and spiritually dead people until his return to the Great Master in 1975. Elijah taught that, Fard had said, "My name is Mahdi; I am God." According to other source, Fard, when asked who he was by the Detroit police, He responded as such: "I am the Supreme Ruler of the Universe.

Prophet Noble Drew Ali

In 1916 AD, a so-called Blackman wearing a red fez worn by Moroccans appeared on street corners of Chicago's South Side to proclaim who the original man is and what is his real name.

He was Noble Drew Ali, born Timothy Drew in North Carolina, Prophet of Islamism and founder of the Moorish Temple of Science. Newark, New Jersey, is where he founded the first Asiatic Temple of Science in 1913. He also established Temples in Pittsburgh and Detroit before he went on to Chicago where the Asiatic Science Temple of America is incorporated. (Under a religious organization)

Noble Drew Ali's main contention was that the people known in America as the so-called Black man woman and child are in reality Moors and Asiatics. Act six of the 'Divine Constitution and By Laws' of the Moorish Science Temple of America reads: "With us all members must proclaim their nationality and their Divine Creed that they may know that they are a part and partial of this said government and that they are not Negroes, Colored Folks, Black People or Ethiopians. Because these names were given by slaveholders in 1779 and lasted until 1865 during the time of slavery but this is a new era of time now. And all men must proclaim their free national name to be recognized by the government in which they live and the nations of the earth, this is the reason Allah the Great God of the Universe ordained Noble Drew Ali, the Prophet to redeem his people from their sinful ways. The Moorish Americans are the descendants of the Ancient Moabites whom inhabited the North Western and South Western shores of Africa also the NE and SE shores of the Americas.

Prophet Noble Drew Ali immediately rallied many Moors to his Temples; with the green 5-pointed star on a red back round as the Asiatic Flag, nothing could stop the movement except the Moors. Taught in the Far East and possessing powerful speeches, with a persuasive manner, and a Native American shrewdness that enabled him to teach the poor, rich, learned and unlettered people, and all who would listen. Most of them remembered the race riots of 1919; all of them had experienced discrimination, segregation and other wrongs. Drew Ali offered them pride and dignity with knowledge of self and God. In 1928, a successful convention provided Noble Drew Ali with an expansion of his Temple activities to other cities. It is not difficult to ascertain just how many Temples resulted, (because of the record keeping by the Moors) in cities like Pittsburgh, Detroit, Charleston, West Virginia, Lansing, Michigan, and Youngstown Ohio. Drew Ali had divinely prepared and published his 'Circle 7 Koran', a book consisting of the life of Jesus, and the science of life in degrees to follow.

The Prophet did business in various oils and teas he had divinely prepared, among them, Moorish Blood Purifier, Bath Compounds and other Moorish remedies that work and that are still in use in Temples of Moorish Science today. Asiatics flocked to the star and crescent; they wore their fezzes on the street and the European stopped treating them with contempt. The Prophet announced that each devoted Moorish American must carry a Nationality card bearing his or her real name with title, signed by the Prophet with an Asiatic Seal. Today Slave names are Amended and "real" ones added with the use of the ninth Amendment of the US Constitution.

The titles are 'El' or 'Bey', signifying Moorish Nobility, the Nationality Card, star and crescent, when displayed to Europeans; some how convince the European that the bearer was an enlightened Moorish American.

The Prophet found independence for the Moors ethical and theoretically. Reports from newspapers wrote about street brawls, threats, insults, and minor violence centering on the Asiatic Americas. Moors were approaching Europeans on the streets, showing their Nationality Cards and Flags, and proclaiming in the name of their Prophet, Noble Drew Ali, and Allah that they "had been freed of European slave names and mindset.

After all of this was done by the Moors, Drew Ali issued the following law in the book called Humanities, 'I hereby warn all Moors that they must cease from all radical or agitating speeches while on their jobs, or in their homes, or on the streets. Stop flashing your cards before Europeans as this only causes confusion. We did not come to cause confusion; our work is to uplift the nation' etc…

Drew Ali's leadership is contested in 1929 by Claude Greene, politician and former butler of Julius Rosenwald, who had previously joined the Asiatic Nation. One day Drew Ali arrived at his office to find that Greene had moved all the furniture outside and had declared himself Grand Sheik. A civil war ensued, each faction enlisting support from temples in other cities. Greene was shot and stabbed to death in his office at the Unity Club on the night of March 15, 1929.

Drew Ali, was arrested as he sat with his wife and a group of Moors, he was defended by Attorneys Aaron Payne and William L. Dawson, and Moorish Americans who had gained political prominence. Sister Nana said that; "The Prophet, from prison, issued a message to the Moorish Americans, To the Heads of All Temples, Islam, I your Prophet, do hereby and now write you a letter as a warning and appeal to your good judgment for the present and the future. Though I am now in custody for you and the movement, it is all right and it is well for all who still believe in my Father God Allah. I have redeemed all of you, and you are saved all of you, the teaching of Allah can save even those who are not with me. I go to bat Monday, May 20, before the Grand Jury. If you are with me, be there. Hold on and keep the faith, and great shall be your reward. Remember my laws and love ye one another. Prefer not a stranger to your brother, Love, Truth, Peace, Freedom and Justice I leave all Moors.

Peace from Your Prophet, Noble Drew Ali

This was Drew Ali's final proclamation, released on bond; he died under mysterious circumstances a few weeks later. One Moor stated that he had succumbed to injuries inflicted by the police during his imprisonment; another Moor stated that, 'he was set upon by Greene and beaten so severely that he never really recovered'. After Drew Ali's death, C. Kirkman Bey held the Moors together. Several of the Prophet's disciples announced that they alone were the rightful inheritor of Drew Ali's leadership. John Givens El (formerly the Prophet's chauffer) and Johnson Bey (who had been imported from Pittsburgh to assist in quelling the Greene revolt) each conceived the idea that the dead Prophet's spirit entered Givens El's body. Johnson, a man of action, invaded the office of Mealy El, another leader of the Moors, and demanded recognition as Grand Sheik. Mealy El demurred and received a terrific mauling.
Johnson then dispatched his men to kidnap C. Kirkman Bey, who had possession of Drew Ali's last will and testament. C. Kirkman Bey's wife surmised that her husband was

detained in Johnson's apartment, directed the police thither. A gun battle ensued in which two police officers and one Moor was killed. Sixty-three Moors were arrested, and Johnson was committed to the State Hospital for the criminally insane where he subsequently died. John Givens El also was apprehended after he forced his way into Attorney Payne's home in search of Drew Ali's papers. Givens is sent to the insane asylum, but was released several years later. In 1941, he was heading a Chicago Temple on East 40th St. and still asserting his claim to the title of Grand Sheik of all Moorish American Science Temples. Givens was one of six contestants, each one a Temple leader and each one designating his own Temple as Temple Number one (1).

Services in each Moorish Science Temple are observed, somewhat by the pattern established by Noble Drew Ali. First, a minor Sheik, a Sheikhs and/or the chairperson reads and explains Drew Ali's Circle 7 Koran. Then follows a more elaborate discourse by the Grand Sheik of the Asiatic Science Temple of America, the whole ceremony punctuated by Christian hymns (The Hymn book was written in 1933) with the words Allah, Drew Ali, and Moslem substituted for God, Christ, and Christian. Friday is observed as a holy day of rest, 'because on a Friday the first man was formed in flesh and on a Friday the first man departed out of the flesh and ascended unto his Father God Allah, for that cause Friday is the Holy Day for Moslems all over the world'. (Divine Constitution and By Laws) Drew Ali considered Marcus Garvey his forerunner (in a relationship to John the Baptist and Jesus); paid tribute to him both in the Circle 7 Koran and in Asiatic Literature, Moorish Americans often honor, and quotes the Jamaican Harbinger 'Marcus Garvey'.

January the 8th, is Prophet Drew Ali's birthday, a special occasion in all Asiatic Science Temples of America, those Moors who can wear full Asiatic regalia do, and there is a feasting and distribution of gifts in celebrations of the Prophet Drew Ali. Guests are invited; speeches take on a scientific and historical tone. The teachings and principals of the Prophet are offered in form of a Nationality Card, for the benefit of those still under the influence of a slave name without a title. The leaders of each of the Temples has striven to build up an organization as powerful as the parent body disrupted by internal warfare also the death of Drew Ali the movement has manage to teach the Prophet's word unchanged.

Father Allah

Clarence Smith was born on <u>Wednesday</u>, February 22, 1928 in Danville, Virginia, the fifth son of Louis and Mary Smith, his sister Bernice and younger brother Harry were born after him to complete the family of seven six boys and one girl. Clarence's mother nicknamed him 'Put' and this is what they called him throughout his early childhood.

The young Put had a childhood in a world and time of segregation and miscegenation. In 1940, Clarence's mother, 'Mary' moved to Harlem New York, and in 1946, Clarence came to join his mother and older brothers. Once in Harlem, his nickname, 'Put' was mistaken for 'Puddin' and from that day forward has name became Puddin.
Puddin performed a number of odd jobs to keep money in his pockets. Among them was a fruit stand that he opened up in Harlem. It was also in Harlem that he developed a

knack for gambling. He played a lot of pool in Harlem also as Puddin and these days got him a reputation as a Pool Shark. In 1950, Mr. C. Smith joined the Army and went to fight in the Korean War. Half a world away and at war did not deter him from the loves of his life, he would send money home regularly, that he had won gambling.

He returned to the US and accepted the teachings of Islam under Elijah Muhummed and joined Temple Number 7, Minister Malcolm X was the leader of Temple 7 in the 1960's. It was in the Temple that he met Akbar (Justice) who would become his closest associate for many years to come, soon after, he was promoted to the position of lieutenant with the responsibility of training the Fruit of Islam (FOI) in Karate, which he had learned while he was in Korea.

In addition, he had a speaking style that was unique, a slow methodical cadence stressing syllables that normally are not. It was hypnotic; the Father was again promoted, this time to the position of student minister. Elijah Muhammad had received word of this fiery young student minister and traveled to New York to meet him, and to bestow him with the name of Abdullah.

In 1963, when the Father was addressing the student minister class he was speaking about what makes rain, hail, snow and earthquakes, he was manifesting his self-style wisdom, that 'all that above is cause by the son man'. The head of the FOI, Captain Joseph, walked into the room and heard what the Father was teaching, he then stopped the meeting, dismissed the men, and spoke with the Father. The Captain told Abdullah that he could not teach what he was teaching here in the temple. It was a time of turmoil in general for the Nation of Islam, Minister Malcolm X himself was given a suspension from the temple, and so Abdullah (The Father) left the temple, Justice would leave with the Father other brothers who understood the reality of Abdullah's teachings.

He removed him self from the temple with lost found lessons (that had so much to do with him developing into a fiery orator), back to the streets of Harlem, teaching, "I is self, self is the true reality, son of man, God" to the masses of youth who have not receive knowledge of self, their people and history. In 1963, the Father left temple number 7, the Father Amended his name from Clarence 13X to Father Allah then went to the streets of Harlem to do God's work, moreover, that was to reach his blind, deaf and dumb people (85%), and from them, raise the 5% Nation.

His first students were Kareem (Black Messiah), Nahiim (Bismii Allah), Uhuru, Kihiem, Al-Jabbar (Prince Allah), Al Jamel, Bilal (Jihad and/or ABG 7), Akbar, and Al Salaam. They called Allah, 'Father' because many of them were the product of broken homes and he was their father, thus the Father taught his First Nine Born. Allah's First Born became very powerful and dynamic young men that brought hundreds of Asiatic youth into the knowledge of self. They became known as Allah's Five Percent Nation.

The Father taught them that they were of the Most High even though they would be considered by some to be the lowest in the wilderness of North America. He taught that they should not be anti-white nor pro-black, but that they should be anti-devilish and pro-righteous, and that they should fear nothing in this world, that even the devil did not fear death, his only fear was of Allah, because he knew not when or how he would come. In addition, that if they were one with Allah, there should be no reason to fear anything in this world. He told them that they did not need guns unless they had the legal paper for them, that their tongue was their sword, and that they could take more heads with the word, than an Army could. Moreover, that he who must live by the gun shall surely die by the gun. The Father did not teach the 5% to fight fire with a tulip, but he taught them not to try to put out a fire with gasoline. The First Born was each required to teach 10 children or people younger than they were and they shall be their fruit. Note: These are the teachings that the Father left for his 5% nation.

Fard

The Problem Book is a degree that was given to Elijah Muhummed by WD Fard in the 1930's. W.D. Fard said; this book would teach the Lost-Found Nation, knowledge in a mathematical way.

1. The uncle of Mr. WD Fard lived in the wilderness of North America and he lived other than his own self, therefore, his pulse beat seventy-eight times per minute and this killed him at forty-five years of age. How many times did, his pulse beat in forty-five years?

2. The wife of Mr. WD Fard's uncle, in the wilderness of North America, weighs other than herself, therefore, she has rheumatism, headaches, pain in all joints, and cannot walk to the store. She is troubled frequently with high blood pressure. Her pulse is nearly eighty times per minute and she died at the age of forty-seven. How many times did her pulse beat in forty-seven years?

3. A sheep contains fourteen square feet of hair. One-tenth of a square inch contains ten thousand hairs. How many will the fourteen square feet contain?
4. One one-hundredth Of a cubic inch contains two hundred million Atoms. How many will fifty square miles contain?

5. The uncle of WD Fard lives in the wilderness of North America and he is living other than himself, therefore, he weighs more than he should at his height and he has high blood pressure. This killed him at the age of forty-four years. The average person breathes three cubic feet of air per hour, but the uncle of WD Fard breathes three and seven-tenths of a cubic foot per hour. How many cubic feet of air did WD Fard's uncle breathe in forty-four years? How many Atoms does he breathe in all of his forty-four years when one one-hundredth of a cubic inch contains two hundred million Atoms?

6. The second uncle of WD Fard, in the wilderness of North America, lived other than himself and, therefore, his blood pressure registered over one hundred thirty-two over one hundred. He had fever, headaches, chills, grippe, hay fever, regular fever, rheumatism; also pain in all joints. He was disturbed with foot ailments and toothaches. His pulse beat

more that eighty-eight times per minute, therefore, he goes to the doctor every day and gets medicine for every day in the year one after each meal, or three times a day. The average person breathes three cubic feet of air per hour, but the second uncle of WD Fard breathed four and one-half cubic feet of air per hour. Five hundred pills equal one pound, so that kills him at the age of forty-six. How many pounds of pills did WD Fard's second uncle use in forty-six years? How many cubic feet of air did he breathe in forty-six years? How much does WD Fard's second uncle get rob of in forty-six years? If twenty pills cost twenty-five cents? (He buys 7 pills a day) How much does this amount to in forty-six years? Once a week, he gives the doctor $2.50 for renewing the prescription. In addition, fifty-two weeks equal one year. So Muhammad wants to know how much money was spent for the pills and Doctors?

7. If one one-hundredth of a cubic inch contains two hundred million Atoms, and if the total Atmosphere weighs eleven and two-thirds quintillion pounds. Then one-third of the eleven and two-thirds quintillion pounds equal how many Atoms? Muhammad cracked one Atom into ten million parts. Then Sheriffs wants to know how much one-third of a cracked Atom weighs?

8. Four quintillion pounds equal the total amount of Atoms. One one-hundredth of a square inch equals two hundred million Atoms. Extract the cube root of three-fourths of a cracked Atom. If a cracked Atom equals one-ten thousandth of one atom, DW Shah wants to know what will be the weight of the cracked Atom.

9. The population of Detroit is one million five hundred thousand people, and there are two hundred and fifty thousand in the original nation. During these hard times for the lack of jobs, not having enough money to buy food, they eat two meals per day. The average person eats four ounces of bread, ten and one-fifth ounces of poison animal, three and one-third ounces or rice, four and one-eighth ounces of other meal helpers.
It is known to the Medical Profession and other wise Muslim Sons that poison animal hurts the mental power; of one-sixtieth of an ounce per every ten ounces of poison animal. If the average person contains seven and one-half ounces of brain, then Muhammad wants to know how long will it take to hurt the seven and one-half ounces at the above eating rates?

If the average person can be robbed successfully of one-third of their brainpower at the above rate, over a 20 year span. Then how long will an animal eater have to wait to destroy said brainpower, at the above rates in 80 years?

10. Lake Erie is nine thousand, nine hundred, sixty square miles and the average depth is one thousand, nine hundred, sixty feet. The uncle of WD Fard lives near this lake in the City of Detroit, therefore, he uses the water from this Lake for all household purposes. A certain European told him not to use too much water if you can help it, so he only used forty gallons per day. Nevertheless, the second uncle of WD Fard is using two hundred gallons of water per day. How long will it take the first and second uncle to empty the Lake using water at the above rates? One cubic foot of water weighs sixty-two and one-half pounds. How many ounces of water are in Lake Erie? Sixteen ounces equal one

pound. How many cubic inches is in Lake Erie? One thousand seven hundred twenty-eight cubic inches equal one foot.

11. The Suez (Zeus) Canal in Egypt is ninety-nine miles long, with a depth of thirty-three feet, and width of one hundred twenty-two feet. The cost to build it sixty-four years ago as of 1933, was one hundred fifty million dollars, Ali has five hundred dollars worth of stock in it at the rate of six and three-fifths percent, now he wants to know how much money he has coming to him at the above rate from 1869 to May 26, 1933. How many ounces of water are in the canal? How many cubic inches are in the canal? One thousand seven hundred twenty-eight cubic inches equal one cubic foot, one cubic foot equals sixty-two and one-half pounds of water, the Nile river, the longest river on the Planet, is four thousand six hundred ninety miles long, and one and three-eight miles wide. How many square miles are in the Nile River? How many square inches are there in the Nile River?

12. The area of our Planet is one hundred ninety-six million, nine hundred forty thousand square miles and she weighs six sex-tillion tons. Shamell wants to know how much does the State of Michigan weigh? Going by the Book of Cave out Of Darkness saying: that the State of Michigan is fifty-seven thousand, nine hundred eighty square miles and has a population of four million, eight hundred forty-two thousand, and two hundred eighty people, one cubic foot of common Earth weighs eighty pounds. If the average European weighs two hundred pounds and the average Asiatic weighs two hundred fifty pounds and there are five hundred thousand Asiatics living in the State of Michigan.

With approximately eight million different livestock on farms, with the average livestock weighing six hundred fifty-nine pounds and the construction of humans is approximately one hundred fifty billion tons. So then, how much does the State of Michigan weigh? How much does the livestock weigh? How much do the Europeans weigh? How much do the Asiatics weigh? How much do the total weights of all weigh?

13. After learning Mathematics, which is I-God and I-God, is Mathematics, it stands true. You can always prove it at no limit of time. Then you must learn to use it and secure some benefit while you are living, that is luxury, money, good homes, friendship in all lifestyles. Sit yourself in Heaven at once!

This is the greatest Desire of your Brothers and Teachers. Now you must speak the language so you can use your Mathematical Theology in the proper Term otherwise you will not be successful unless you do speak well, for he or her knows all about you. There are 26 letters in the Alphabets, if a student learns one letter per day, then how long will it take him to learn the twenty-six letters?

14. The University of Al-Azhar, in Cairo, has a student population of thirty-six hundred; all but one-tenth taking other than his own Language, three-tenths taking Construction Engineering, two-tenths taking Civil Engineering, three-tenths taking Mechanical Engineering, and the rest taking Teacher-ship. One, one hundred and eighty-fifth of one had more than eight absent charges to their credit. Therefore, at the end of their Courses,

they do not receive diplomas. How many were Construction Engineers? How many were Civil Engineers? How many were Mechanical Engineers? How many were Teachers? How many were in number that did not receive Diplomas? The Law of Islam prescribes that a Student shall not be given a diploma if he has eight or more absent charges to his account.

15. The planet Earth has a population of forty-eight hundred million people as of 1933. Forty-four hundred million are the Asiatic nations and four hundred million are the European civilizations. We need to live in peace but some of the Europeans do not want to live with the Asiatics. What would be the exact number of persons of each European against the Asiatics?

After learning Mathematics, it stands true you can always prove it in no limit of time. Then you must learn to use it and secure some benefit while you are living, that is luxury, money, good homes, friendship in all lifestyles.

It is also known to the civilized world that ten ounces of the poison animal destroys three one-hundredths percent of the beauty appearance of a person. Then Muhammad wants to know how long will it take to destroy the whole, one hundred percent of the beauty appearance at the above eating rates? There are ten numbers in the Mathematical Language. Then how long will it take a Student to learn the whole ten numbers (at the above rate)? The average person speaks four hundred words considered well we should learn to speak 800 words very well and on to 1000, how long will it take to learn 900 words at the above rate? Note: Some said, Fard used this formula to help Asiatics in the 1930's.

Master Fard Muhummed born February 26, 1877 in the Holy City, Mecca, Master Fard Muhummed came to North America, in the year 1910 AD looking for one from among the so-called black people to teach, the "word of God" he stated that "it must be one from among them" to give and receive light on the square. He signed His name W.F. Muhammad, which stands for Wallace Fard Muhammad. 'He came to the wilderness' of North America and found Mr. Elijah Poole, (One from among the so-called back people) He began teaching him the knowledge of him self, of God and the devil, of the measurement of the earth, of other planets, and of the civilizations of some of the planets other than earth in 1930 AD. He went from door to door selling clothing and accessories, as well as artifacts. These, he claimed, were like those the ancestors (of the so-called black man) wore and used. As he peddled his goods, he told tales about the so-called blacks of Africa that entranced his customers, this led to informal gatherings in homes in which he told the Asiatics about their land of origin. At first, his talks focused on the so-called black man's history, culture, diet, politics and religion.

Eventually, he introduced the Asiatics to the Qur'an; his teachings denounce the European race for the wrongs they have done to the so-called Black man. His audiences became so large that they could no longer meet in homes. A hall was rented, and named, 'The Temple of Islam', Fard soon built his following into a tightly knit culture that looked to him as their leader.

He established a University, which emphasized the teaching of Math and Astronomy. Fard began a Muslim Girls Training and General Civilization Class that continues to teach the principles of home economics and how to be proper wives and mothers to this day. He instituted a Para-military unit called 'Fruit of Islam' (FOI) to teach military tactics and Wing Chung for the predicted day that the some European-Americans would not tolerate their growth and prosperity.

He also set up the office of 'The Ministers of Islam', in three short years, Fard had acquired some 7,000 followers. Under the direction of The Ministers of Islam and the Labors, the Temple continued to prosper. One of Fard's early disciples, Elijah Poole (some say Elijah Poole Bey), was given the Muslim name Elijah Muhammad, and was ultimately named as the chief Minister.

In June of 1934, only four years after he made his first appearance in Detroit to Elijah, WD Fard completely and mysteriously disappeared.

SONS OF DESTINY
Chapter 11

Albert Einstein

On March 14, 1879, Albert Einstein is born, the son of a Jewish electrical engineer in Germany. Einstein's theories of special and general relativity drastically altered man's view of the universe, and his work in particle and energy theory helped make possible quantum mechanics and, ultimately, the atomic bomb.

After a childhood in Germany and Italy, Einstein studied physics and mathematics at the Federal Polytechnic Academy in Switzerland. He became a Swiss citizen and in 1905 is awarded a Ph.D. from the University of Zurich. That year, he published five theoretical papers that were to have a profound effect on the development of modern physics.

In the first of these, titled "On a Heuristic Viewpoint Concerning the Production and Transformation of Light," Einstein theorized that light is made up of individual quanta (photons) that demonstrate particle-like-properties while collectively behaving like a wave.

The hypothesis, an important step in the development of quantum theory, was arrived at through Einstein's examination of the photoelectric effect, a phenomenon in which some solids emit electrically charged particles when struck by light. This work would later earn him the 1921 Nobel Prize in Physics.
In the second paper, he devised a new method of counting and determining the size of the atoms and molecules in a given space, and in the a third paper he offered a mathematical explanation for the constant erratic movement of particles suspended in a fluid, known as Brownian motion. These two papers provided indisputable evidence of the existence of atoms, which at the time was still disputed by a few scientists.

Einstein's fourth groundbreaking scientific work of 1905 addressed what he termed his special theory of relativity. In special relativity, time and space are not absolute, but relative to the motion of the observer. Thus, two observers traveling at great speeds in regard to each other would not necessarily observe simultaneous events in time at the same moment, nor necessarily agree in their measurements of space. In Einstein's theory, the speed of light, which is the limiting speed of any body having mass, is constant in all frames of reference. In the fifth paper that year, an exploration of the mathematics of special relativity, Einstein announced that mass and energy were equivalent and could be calculated with an equation, $E = mc^2$.

Although the public was not quick to embrace his revolutionary science, Einstein was welcomed into the circle of Europe's most eminent physicists and given professorships in Zurich, Prague, and Berlin. In 1916, he published "The Foundation of the General Theory of Relativity," which proposed that gravity, as well as motion, can affect the intervals of time and of space. According to Einstein, gravitation is not a force, as Isaac Newton had argued, but a curved field in the space-time continuum, created by the presence of mass. An object of very large gravitational mass, such as the sun, would therefore appear to warp space and time around it, which could be demonstrated by observing starlight on its way to the earth. In 1919, astronomers studying a solar eclipse verified predictions Einstein made in the general theory of relativity, and he became an overnight celebrity. Later, other predictions of general relativity, such as a shift in the orbit of the planet Mercury and the probable existence of black holes, were confirmed by scientists. During the next decade, Einstein made continued contributions to quantum theory and began work on a unified field theory, which he hoped would encompass quantum mechanics and his own relativity theory as a grand explanation of the workings of the universe.

As a world-renowned public figure, he became increasingly political, speaking out against militarism and rearmament. In his native Germany, this made him an unpopular figure, and after Nazi leader Adolf Hitler became chancellor of Germany in 1933 Einstein renounced his German citizenship and left the country.

He later settled in the US, where he accepted a post at the Institute for Advanced Study in Princeton, NJ. He would remain there for the rest of his life, working on his unified field theory and relaxing by sailing on a local lake or playing his violin. He became an American citizen in 1940. In 1939, despite his lifelong pacifist beliefs, he agreed to write to President Franklin D. Roosevelt on behalf of a group of scientists who were concerned with American inaction in the field of atomic-weapons research. Like the other scientists, he feared sole German possession of such a weapon. He played no role, however, in the subsequent Manhattan Project and the later deplored use of atomic bombs against Japan. After the war, he called for the establishment of a world government that would control nuclear technology and prevent future-armed conflicts.

In 1950, he published his unified field theory, which was quietly criticized as a failure. A unified explanation of gravitation, subatomic phenomena, and electromagnetism remains elusive today. Albert Einstein, one of the most creative minds in human history, died in Princeton in the year 1955.

Adolf Hitler

Adolf Hitler is reviled as one of history's greatest villains. Hitler becomes Fuhrer, August 2, 1934 with the death of German President Paul von Hindenburg; Chancellor Adolf Hitler becomes absolute dictator of Germany under the title of Fuehrer, or "Leader." The German army took an oath of allegiance to its new commander-in-chief, and the last remnants of Germany's democratic government were dismantled for Hitler's Third Reich. Hitler assured people that the Third Reich would last for a thousand years, but Hitler would last just 11 years. Adolf Hitler was born in Austria, in 1889. As a young man, he aspired to be a painter, but he received little public recognition and lived in poverty in Vienna, of German descent, he came to detest Austria as a 'patchwork nation' of various ethnic groups, and in 1913, he moved to the German city of Munich in the state of Bavaria. After a year of drifting, he found direction as a German soldier in World War I, and was decorated for his bravery on the battlefield.

The story goes, he was in a military hospital in 1918, recovering from a mustard gas attack that left him temporarily blind, when Germany surrendered. He was appalled by Germany's defeat, which he blamed on 'the enemies within' chiefly the German communists, Jews, and he was enraged by the 'punitive peace settlement forced on Germany by the victorious Allies'. He remained in the German army after the war, and as intelligence agent, he was 'ordered to report on subversive activities in Munich's political parties'.

He then joined the tiny German Workers Party, made up of embittered army veterans, as the group's seventh member. Hitler was put in charge of the party's propaganda, and in 1920, he assumed leadership of the organization, changing its name to 'National Socialist German Workers' Party', which was abbreviated to 'Nazi's. The party's socialist orientation was a ploy to attract working-class support. Nevertheless, the economic views of the party were overshadowed by the Nazis' fervent nationalism, which blamed Jews, communists, the Treaty of Versailles, and Germany's ineffectual democratic government etc., for the country's devastated economy. In 1920, the ranks of Hitler's Bavarian based Nazi party swelled with resentful Germans. A paramilitary organization, the Sturmabteilung (SA), was formed to protect the Nazis and intimidate their political opponents, and the party adopted the ancient symbol of the swastika as its emblem. In November 1923, after the German government resumed the payment of war reparations to Britain and France, the Nazis launched the 'Beer Hall Putsch' an attempt at seizing the German government by force.
However, the uprising was immediately suppressed, and Hitler was arrested and sentenced to five years in prison for treason. Imprisoned he spent his time there dictating his autobiography. (See **My Struggle**)

Political pressure from the Nazis forced the Bavarian government to commute Hitler's sentence, and he was released after nine months. However, Hitler emerged to find his party disintegrated. An upturn in the economy further reduced popular support of the party, and for several years, Hitler was forbidden to make speeches in Bavaria and elsewhere in Germany. The onset of the Great Depression in 1929 brought a new opportunity for the Nazis to solidify their power. Hitler and his followers set about reorganizing the party as a fanatical mass movement, and won financial backing from business leaders, for whom the Nazis promised an end to labor agitation. In the 1930 election, the Nazis won six million votes, making the party the second largest in Germany. Two years later, Hitler challenged Paul von Hindenburg for the presidency, but the 84-year-old president defeated Hitler. Although the Nazis suffered a decline in votes during the November 1932 election, Hindenburg agreed to make Hitler chancellor in January 1933, 'hoping that Hitler could be brought to heel' as a member of his cabinet. However, Hindenburg underestimated Hitler, as a new chancellor his first act was to exploit the burning of the Reichstag parliament building as a pretext for calling 'general elections'. The police under Nazi Hermann Goering suppressed much of the party's opposition before the election, and the Nazis won a bare majority. Shortly after, Hitler took on dictatorial power through the Enabling Acts. Chancellor Hitler immediately set about arresting and executing political opponents, and even purged the Nazis' own SA paramilitary organization in a successful effort to win support from the German army.

With the death of President Hindenburg on August 2, 1934, Hitler united the chancellorship and presidency under the new title of Fuehrer. As the economy, improved, popular support for Hitler's regime became strong, 'and a cult of Fuehrer worship was propagated by Hitler's capable propagandists'. German remilitarization and state-sanctioned anti-Jewish propaganda drew criticism from home and abroad, but the foreign powers could not 'fail to stem the rise of Nazi Germany'. In 1938, Hitler implemented his 'plans for world domination' with the annexation of Austria, and in 1939, 'he seized all of Czechoslovakia'.

Hitler's invasion of Poland on September 1, 1939, 'Germany and France are at war'. Hitler's war machine won a series of stunning victories, conquering 'the great part of continental Europe'. However, the tide turned in 1942 during Germany's invasion of the USSR. By early 1945, 'Great Briton' and America were closing in on Germany from the west, the Soviets from the east, and Hitler was holed up in a' bunker under the chancellery in Berlin'. On April 30, with the Soviets less than a mile from his headquarters, Hitler 'committed suicide' with 'Eva Braun', whom he 'married' the night before. Hitler left Germany devastated with the Allies divided after that became the 'Cold War'. (See U.S. and USSR cold war)

Ben-Gurion

On May 14, 1948, in Tel Aviv, Jewish Agency Chairman David Ben-Gurion proclaims the State of Israel, establishing the first Jewish state. Ben-Gurion pronounced the words "We hereby proclaim the establishment of the Jewish state in Palestine, to be called Israel." 'Weapons could be heard from fighting that broke out between Jews and Arabs immediately following the British army withdrawal earlier that day'. 'Egypt launched an air assault against Israel that evening'. Despite a blackout in TelAviv, and the expected Arab invasion, Jews joyously celebrated the birth of their new nation, especially after word was received that the United States had recognized the Jewish state. At midnight, the State of Israel officially came into being upon termination of the British mandate in Palestine. Ottoman controlled Palestine, was chosen as the most desirable location for a Jewish state, and Herzl unsuccessfully petitioned the Ottoman government for a Charter. After the failed Russian Revolution of 1905, growing numbers of Eastern European and Russian Jews began to immigrate to Palestine, joining the few thousand Jews who had arrived earlier. The Jewish settlers insisted on the use of Hebrew as their spoken language. With the collapse of the Ottoman Empire during World War I, Britain took over Palestine. In 1917, Britain issued the "Balfour Declaration. Although protested by the Arab states, the Balfour Declaration was included in the British mandate over Palestine, which was authorized by the League of Nations in 1922. Because of Arab opposition to the establishment of any Jewish state in Palestine, British rule continued from 1920 thru 1930. Beginning in 1929, Arabs and Jews openly fought in Palestine, and Britain attempted to limit Jewish immigration. Jewish groups employed terrorism against British forces in Palestine, which they thought had 'betrayed the Zionist cause'. At the end of World War II, in 1945, the United States took up the 'Zionist' cause. Britain, unable to find a practical solution, referred the problem to the United Nations, which in November 1947 'voted to partition Palestine'.

The Jews were to possess some of Palestine; they made up about half of Palestine's population. The Palestinian Arabs, aided by volunteers from other countries, fought with the Jewish forces, by May 14, 1948, the Jewish forces had secured full control of their U.N. allocated share of Palestine and some Arab territory. On May 14, Britain withdrew with the expiration of its mandate, and the State of Israel was proclaimed. The next day, forces from Egypt, Tran Jordan, Syria, Lebanon, and Iraq invaded. The Israelis, managed to fight off the Arabs and then seize key territories, such as Galilee, the Palestinian coast, and a strip of territory connecting the coastal region to the western section of Jerusalem. In 1949, U.N. brokered cease-fires left the State of Israel in permanent control of this conquered territory. The departure of hundreds of thousands of Palestinian Arabs from Israel during the war left the country with a substantial Jewish majority. During the third Arab/Israeli conflict, the Six-Day War of 1967 Israel greatly increased its borders, capturing from Jordan, Egypt, and Syria the Old City of Jerusalem, the Sinai Peninsula, the Gaza Strip, the West Bank, and the Golan Heights. In 1979, Israel and Egypt signed an historic peace agreement in which Israel returned the Sinai in exchange for Egyptian recognition and peace. Israel and the Palestine Liberation Organization (PLO) signed a major peace accord in 1993, which envisioned the gradual implementation of Palestinian self-government in the West Bank and Gaza Strip.
The Israeli-Palestinian peace process moved slowly, however, and in 2000 major fighting between Israelis and Palestinians resumed in Israel and the occupied territories. Until this day, this conflict has not been resolved.

Brigham Young

After 17 months and many miles of travel, Brigham Young leads 148 Mormon pioneers into Utah's Valley of the Great Salt Lake. Gazing over the parched earth of the remote location, Young declared, "This is the place," and the pioneers began preparations for the thousands of Mormon migrants who would follow. Seeking religious and political freedom, the Mormons began planning their great migration from the east after the murder of Joseph Smith, the Christian sect's founder and first leader. Joseph Smith was born in Sharon, Vermont, in 1805. In 1827, he declared that a Christian angel named Moroni, who showed him an ancient Hebrew text that had been lost for 1,500 years, had visited him. The holy text, supposedly engraved on gold plates by a Native American prophet named Mormon in the fifth century A.D., told the story of Israelite peoples who had lived in America in ancient times. During the next few years, Smith dictated an English translation of this text to his wife and other scribes, and in 1830 ace The Book of Mormon was published. In the same year, Smith founded the Church of Christ--later known as the Church of Jesus Christ of Latter-day Saints--in Fayette, New York. The religion rapidly gained converts, and Smith set up Mormon communities in Ohio, Missouri, and Illinois. However, the Christian sect was also heavily criticized for its unorthodox practices, which included polygamy. In 1844, the threat of mob violence prompted Smith to call out a militia in the Mormon town of Nauvoo, Illinois. He was charged with treason by Illinois authorities and imprisoned with his brother Hyrum in the Carthage city jail. On June 27, 1844, an anti-Mormon mob with blackened faces stormed in and murdered the brothers.

Two years later, Smith's successor, Brigham Young, led an exodus of persecuted Mormons from Nauvoo along the western wagon trails in search of a sanctuary in 'a place on this earth that nobody else wants'. The expedition, more than 10,000 pioneers strong, set up camp in present-day western Iowa while Young led a vanguard company across the Rocky Mountains to investigate Utah's Great Salt Lake Valley, an arid and isolated spot devoid of human presence.

On July 22, 1947, most of the party reached the Great Salt Lake, but Young, delayed by illness, did not arrive until July 24. Upon viewing the land, he immediately confirmed the valley to be the new homeland of the Latter-day Saints. Within days, Young and his companions began building the future Salt Lake City at the foot of the Wasatch Mountains. Later that year, Young rejoined the main body of pioneers in Iowa, who named him president and prophet of the church. Having formally inherited the authority of Joseph Smith, he led thousands of more Mormons to the Great Salt Lake in 1848. Other large waves of Mormon pioneers followed. By 1852, 16,000 Mormons had come to the valley, some in wagons and some dragging handcarts. After early difficulties, Salt Lake City began to flourish.

By 1869, 80,000 Mormons had made the trek to their promised land. In 1850, President Millard Fillmore named Brigham Young the first governor of the U.S. territory of Utah, and the territory enjoyed relative autonomy for several years. Relations became strained, however, when reports reached Washington that Mormon leaders were disregarding federal law and had publicly sanctioned the practice of polygamy.

In 1857, President James Buchanan removed Young, who had 20 wives, from his position as governor and sent U.S. Army troops to Utah to establish federal authority. Young died in Salt Lake City in 1877 and was succeeded by John Taylor as president of the Church. Tensions between the territory of Utah and the federal government continued until Wilford Woodruff, the new president of the Mormon Church, issued his Manifesto in 1890, renouncing the traditional practice of polygamy and reducing the domination of the church over Utah communities. Six years later, the territory of Utah entered the Union as the 45th state.

ASIATIC DEGREES
Teachings of the 31 Masters
Chapter 12

1. Face your fears, or they will climb over your back.
2. To know a thing well, know its limits, only when pushed beyond its tolerance is its true nature seen, do not depend only on theory if your life is at stake.
3. Logic moves blindly.
4. The slave makes an awful master.
5. Never choose a course just because it offers the opportunity for a dramatic gesture, awakening of your true self, this is one hundred and twenty times three.
6. Time does not count itself, you have only to look at a circle and this is apparent.
7. What does a mirror look at in a mirror, you will know; you will be looking at your self, as you look at your self.
8. The greatest relevancy can become irrelevant in the space of a heartbeat; Asiatics should look upon such moments with joy.
9. The best music imitates life in a compelling way, if it imitates a dream, it must be a dream of life, otherwise, there is no place, where we can connect, and our plugs do not fit.
10. The past must be re-interpreted by the present.
11. Never, follow a leader without asking your own questions.
12. Memory never recaptures reality, memory reconstructs, and all reconstructions change the original, becoming external frames of reference that inevitably fall short.
13. Complexity hides within complexity; those who cannot remember the past are condemned to repeat it. The unclouded eye is better, no matter what it sees.
14. The writing of history is largely a process of diversion; most historical accounts distract attention from the secret influences behind great events.
15. You are open to whatever the universe may do, your brain is a response tool, keyed to what ever your senses display.
16. Corruption wears infinite disguises. Have they not practiced deception? Vulnerabilities can be created; subtleties are another kind of weapon, a feigned weakness to deflect your enemies and lead them into traps.
17. Your patterns should not follow an acceptable path! Let them think they understand your power and then shoot off in a new direction.
18. Bureaucracies always become voracious aristocracies after they attain commanding power, you see the major flaws in government arise from a fear of making radical internal changes even though a need is clearly seen. Education is no substitute for intelligence,

that elusive quality is defined only in part by puzzle solving abilities. It is in the creation of new puzzles that reflects what your senses report that you round out the definition.

19. A stone is heavy and the sand is weighty; but a fool's wrath is heavier than they both are. One does not risk everything to settle a score prematurely; speed is a device of Shaitan, even addicts dream of freedom.

20. Man is the embodiment of universal entropy. Look for the one answer to all things, because you cannot minister to infinity!

21. It is our pattern not to offer violence for violence, violence builds more violence and the pendulum swings until the violent ones are shattered.

22. Man remains a rebel; he follows his own desires the way he does with his forbidden lovers. Good! The Asiatic man needs such rebellions, the way of the Emperor without Clothes; the rebel is the child that the nakedness was only apparent too.

23. Politics is the art of appearing candid and completely open while concealing as much as possible. Democracy is susceptible to being led astray by having scapegoats paraded in front of the electorate. That is why people do not vote, instinct will tell them it is useless, governments that perpetuate themselves long enough under that belief always become packed with corruption.

24. The Universe is under God. It is one thing, a wholeness against which all separations may be identified.

25. The Asiatic Mother must combine the seductive wiles of a courtesan with untouchable majesty of a virgin goddess, holding these attributes in tension so long as the powers of her youth endure.
For when youth and beauty have gone, she will find that the place between once occupied by tension, has become a wellspring of cunning and resourcefulness.

26. Asiatics must never submit to animals.

27. A world is supported by four things, the learning of the wise, the justice of the great, the prayers of the righteous and the valor of the brave, but all of these are as nothing, without a ruler who knows the art of ruling. You, Asiatic Man, descendant of kings and queens, sons and daughters of a God, you must learn to rule.
It's something your ancestors knew. A process cannot be understood by stopping it, understanding must move with the flow of it, the process must join it, and flow with it.

28. Any road followed precisely to its end leads precisely nowhere.

29. Climb the mountain just a little bit to test that it's a mountain, from the top of the mountain; you can see the entire mountain.

30. The proximity of a desirable thing tempts one to overindulgence, on that path lays danger.

31. Phi = 1.618 in the study between male and female honeybees as in a community of bees, the female bees always out number the male bees. If you divide the number of female bees by the number of male bees in any beehive in the world, you will always get the same number (1.618). Sunflower seeds grow in opposing spirals and the ratio of each rotation's diameter to the next is 1.618. This is true in spiral pinecone petals, leaf arrangements on plant stalks, insect segmentation and all this display has the astonishing obedience to the divine proportion. The body always equals Phi, measure the distance from the tip of your head to the floor, then divide that by the distance from your belly button to the floor and you get phi. Measure the distance from your shoulder to your

fingertip, and then divide it by the distance from your elbow to your fingertips Phi again, hip to floor divided by knee to floor Phi again. Finger joints toes spinal divisions all are Phi, your body is a tribute to the Divine proportion, the chaos of the universe has an underlying order, and Phi is the building block of the universe. These are the illusions of a popular history which a successful religion must promote: Evil men never prosper, only the brave deserve the fair, honesty is the best policy, actions speak louder than words, virtue always triumphs, a good deed is its own reward, any bad human can be reformed, religious talismans protect one from demon possession, only females understand the ancient mysteries and the rich are doomed to unhappiness. The concepts of progress acts as a protective mechanism to shield us from the terrors of the future.

The Child Square and 90 Degrees
Nine Months from Conception Too Birth

The term Moslem implies the works of nature involving the body, from conception to birth, on the right angel motion or square of 90°. Let us consider how that which takes place in one day after birth can spread its influence over 365 and 1/4 days of life, as the earth rotates around the sun.

As velocities, increase there is a definite slowing down of time the exact amount being determined by the transformation, similarly, as velocities slow down there is a definite speeding up of time. Man has an electromagnetic form, electromagnetic waves when radiated move with the velocity of light. In other words, in man's electromagnet form are velocities greater than those of ordinary physical substance, but which are not as great as the 186,173 miles per second or the speed light travels in space. The great circle of the sun comprises 360° squared by the number nine. Nine goes boom, or blows up when 360° is divided by 9, this is equal to 40° this is the number 40, which involves the 40 days and 40 nights of Noah.

The First Month of the Year

Aries is the First month of the New Year, in harmony with the Rising Sun in the Northern Hemisphere, on the Tropic of Cancer, which occurs every year on March 20/21...and ushers in the Spring Season. The Secret of the Number 9 Knowledge or Aries is the first month of the year. The 12 signs of the Zodiac involving Man, Woman, Child and the secrets of the number nine is important as the letters of the Alphabet, which qualify the babies to read and write from Conception.
Conception always occurs while the rays of the Sun is in a certain sign of the Zodiac and the child is born nine months later while the rays of the sun is in another sign of the Zodiac on earth. For example:

1. If conception occurs while the Sun is in the sign Leo, between July 23rd and August 23rd, the child is born when the Sun enters the sign Aries between March 21st and April 19th.

2. If conception occurs while the Sun is in the sign Virgo, between August 24th and September 23rd, the child is born when the Sun enters the sign Taurus between April 20th and May 20th.

3. If conception occurs while the Sun is in the sign Libra, between September 24 and October 22, the child is born when the Sun enters the sign Gemini between May 21st and June 21st.

4. If conception occurs while the Sun is in the sign Scorpio between October 23rd and November 21st, the child is born when the Sun enters the sign Cancer between June 22nd and July 22nd.

5. If conception occurs while the Sun is in the sign Sagittarius between November 22nd and December 20th, the child is born when the Sun enters the sign Leo between July 23rd and August 23rd.

6. If conception occurs while the Sun is in the sign Capricorn between December 21st and January 18th, the child is born when the Sun enters the sign Virgo between August 24th and September 23rd.

7. If conception occurs while the Sun is in the sign Aquarius between January 19th and February 19th, the child is born when the Sun enters the sign Libra between September 24th and October 22nd.

8. If conception occurs while the Sun is in the sign Pisces, between February 20th and March 20th, the child is born when the Sun enters the sign Scorpio between October 23rd and November 21st.

9. If conception occurs while the rays of the Sun is in the sign Aries, between March 21st and April 19th the child is born when the rays of the Sun enter the sign Sagittarius between November 22nd and December 20th.

10. If conception occurs while the rays of the Sun is in the sign Aries, between April 20th and May 20th the child is born when the Sun enters the sign Capricorn between December 21st and January 18th.

11. If conception occurs while the Sun is in the sign Gemini, between May 21st and June 21st, the child is born when the Sun enters the sign Aquarius between January 19th and February 19th.

12. If conception occurs while the Sun is in the sign Cancer, from June 22nd thru July 22nd, the child is born when the Sun enters the sign Pisces between February 20th and March 20th. There are 88 constellations visible from the earth, 12 of those are of the zodiac. The zodiac is a narrow zone on either side of the ecliptic. The 12 signs of the zodiac are Aries, Taurus, Gemini, Cancer, Leo, Virgo, Libra, Scorpius, Sagittarius, Capricornus, Aquarius and Pisces. There is also a 13th Zodiacal Constellation called Ophiuchus the Serpent Holder. Zodiacal constellations do not stay in the sky for only one day, they are in the sky for about a month.

Ophiuchus appears during the first half of December, about 1 in 20 people are really born under the sign of Ophiuchus. In fact, Ophiuchus is a Sun sign in the Solar Zodiac, the Sun can be seen against the stars of Ophiuchus between the 30th of November and the 17th of December. The dates of the cusps move from one year to the next, sometimes they are quoted as starting December 1st to December 18th. This concludes in brief the applied key of the 12 signs of the Zodiac involving the womb of man and the understanding seeds the number 9, also nine months, from conception to birth. This process of simple scientific universal fact has proven that every child is born while the Sun Earth and Moon etc, are passing through one of the 12 signs of the Zodiac and that the sign under which children are born governs their lives from the cradle to the grave. That which cannot be proven by mathematical reasoning, is dangerous to the Asiatics in the US and the world over. During the nine months from conception to birth, the child in the womb, has passed through the nine cosmic regions or signs, in harmony with the Sun Moon and Stars, from which it molds its physical form, brain, memory and characteristics; qualified for cultivation as it slowly grows up during life. If women on a national scale possessed the applied knowledge of the secrets of the number nine, they would be supremely qualified to educate their original children to the practical side of life during the nine months form maturity to conception or birth. Then there would be no need for the institutions of religious mystery worship, idol or image god, jailhouses, prisons and insane institutions would not be needed for there would be no racial hatred or crime.

The secrets of the number nine and the 12 signs of the Zodiac involving man, woman and child, from conception to birth, is referred to in the Book of John, Revelations, as the opening of the 'Seven Seals' from which has marked the very end of mystery, Theology the control of the AB-Originals man woman and child or the Asiatics of the united States of America who have been labeled "Negro, Colored, Black, African American, Afro American, Coon, Shine, Brethren, and you Folks," by the Sociologists of the Roman Cross Order. I assert that the present grown-ups, or 85% of both European and Asiatics in North America will not turn loose the pale image "Christ" doctrine and the Church, with its various denominations, until the united States of America has undergone its bath of wisdom, which is now in the making.

Cleopatra

Cleopatra, born in 69 BC, was made Cleopatra VII, Queen of Egypt, upon the death of her father, Ptolemy XII, in 51 BC, her brother was made King Ptolemy XIII at the same time, and the siblings ruled Egypt under the formal title of husband and wife. Cleopatra and Ptolemy were members of the Macedonian dynasty that governed Egypt since the death of Alexander the Great in 323 BC. To further her influence over the Egyptian people, she was also proclaimed the daughter of Ra, the God of the Sun. Cleopatra fell into dispute with her brother, and civil war erupted in 48 BC Rome, was also beset by civil war at the time. Just as Cleopatra was preparing to attack her brother with a large Arab army, the Roman civil war spilled into Egypt. Pompey the Great, defeated by Julius Caesar in Greece, fled to Egypt seeking solace but was immediately murdered by agents of Ptolemy XIII, Caesar arrived in Alexandria soon after and, finding his enemy dead, decided to restore order in Khamet.
During the preceding century, Rome had exercised increasing control over the rich Egyptian kingdom, and Cleopatra sought to advance her political aims by winning the favor of Caesar. She traveled to the royal palace in Alexandria and was allegedly carried to Caesar rolled in a rug, which was offered as a gift. Cleopatra, beautiful and alluring, captivated the powerful Roman leader, and he agreed to intercede in the Egyptian civil war on her behalf. (See J.A. Rogers)

In 47 BC, Ptolemy XIII was killed after a defeat against Caesar's forces, and Cleopatra was made dual ruler with another brother, Ptolemy XIV. Julius and Cleopatra spent several amorous weeks together, and then Caesar departed for Asia Minor, where he declared 'Veni, vidi, vici' (I came, I saw, I conquered), after putting down a rebellion. In June 47 BC, Cleopatra bore a son, whom was Caesar's and named Caesarion, meaning little Caesar. Upon Caesar's triumphant return to Rome, Cleopatra and Caesarion joined him there. Under the auspices of negotiating a treaty with Rome, Cleopatra lived discretely in a villa that Caesar owned outside the capital. After Caesar was assassinated in March 44 BC, she returned to Egypt. Soon after, Ptolemy XIV died, and the queen made her son co-ruler with her as Ptolemy XV Caesar. With Julius Caesar's murder, Rome again fell into civil war, which was temporarily resolved in 43 BC, with the formation of the second triumvirate, made up of Octavian, Caesar's great-nephew Mark Antony, a general at the time and Lepidus, a Roman political leader.

Antony took up the administration of the eastern provinces of the Roman Empire, and he summoned Cleopatra to Tarsus, in Asia Minor, to answer charges that she had aided his enemies. Cleopatra sought to seduce Antony, as she had Caesar before him, and in 41 BC, arrived in Tarsus on a magnificent river barge, dressed as Venus, the Roman Goddess of Love. Successful in her efforts, Antony returned with her to Alexandria, where they spent the winter. In 40 BC, Antony returned to Rome and married Octavian's sister Octavia in an effort to mend his strained alliance with Octavian. In 37 BC, Antony separated from Octavia and traveled east, arranging for Cleopatra to join him in Syria. In their time apart, Cleopatra had borne him twins, a son and a daughter, the lovers were then married, which violated the Roman law.

Antony's disastrous military campaign against Parthia in 36 BC, further reduced his prestige, but in 34 BC, he was more successful against Armenia. To celebrate the victory, he staged a triumphal procession through the streets of Alexandria, in which he and Cleopatra sat on golden thrones, and Caesarion and their children were given imposing royal titles.

After several more years of tension, Octavian declared war against Cleopatra, and therefore Antony, in 31 BC, enemies of Octavian rallied to Antony's side, but Octavian's brilliant military commanders gained early successes against his forces. On September 2, 31 BC, their fleets clashed at Actium in Greece. After heavy fighting, Cleopatra broke from the engagement and set course for Egypt with 60 of her ships. Antony then broke through the enemy line and followed her. The disheartened fleet that remained surrendered to Octavian. One week later, Antony's land forces surrendered.
Although they had suffered a decisive defeat, it was nearly a year before Octavian reached Alexandria and again defeated Antony. In the aftermath of the battle, Cleopatra took refuge in the mausoleum she had commissioned for herself. Antony, informed that Cleopatra was dead, stabbed himself with his sword. Before he died, another messenger arrived, saying Cleopatra still lived. Antony had himself carried to Cleopatra's retreat, where he died after bidding her to make her peace with Octavian. When the triumphant Roman arrived, she attempted to seduce him, but he resisted her charms. Rather than fall under Octavian's domination, Cleopatra committed suicide on August 30, 30 BC.

Octavian then executed her son Caesarion, annexed Egypt into the Roman Empire, and used Cleopatra's treasure to pay off his veterans. In 27 BC, Octavian became Augustus. He ruled the Roman Empire until his death in 14 AD, at the age of 75. (See J.A. Rogers)

OSIRIS
Chapter 13

Osiris is the sun, his complexion is that of a ripe Olive and his hair is woolly. He is included in a slaughter of the innocents ordered by Typhon from which he escaped. His legitimacy was proved by numerous miracles. Some of his doctrines appear in the Book of the Dead or the Coming Forth by Day and Night, the number of his disciples was 12 he was crucified on the vernal equinox, he descended to hell where he remained 3 days and nights to judge the dead and to rise again and ascended bodily to heaven.

Rotation Sphericity

Al original man gave the first proof of the Sun's rotation and shape. He noted the Sun's roundness and saw that the apparent motion of sunspots in parallel lines with diminished movement at the limbs could be explained if the spots were on the surface of a sphere rotating from east to west. The equator is rotating faster than the poles. Unlike some stars, which rotate rapidly and are strongly flattened oblate spheroids, the Sun is a slow rotator and is so nearly spherical that it is uncertain whether any flattening can be detected. A polar diameter 70 kilometers less than the equatorial diameter has been suggested by some observations. Asiatics have found that most of the matter in the Universe is concentrated in galaxies. Paradoxically, they also have discovered from studying galaxies that the Universe may contain large quantities of mass in a form not observable in galactic systems.

The dominant motion in the disks of normal spiral galaxies is differential galactic rotation, with the random motions of stars being relatively small and that of the atomic and molecular gas smaller still. The rotation curves of almost all well studied spiral galaxies become flat at large radial distances, Aries (The Ram) in astronomy, zodiacal constellation lying between Pisces and Taurus, at about three hour's right ascension, coordinate on the celestial sphere analogous to longitude on the Earth, and 20° north declination, angular distance from the celestial equator.

The Ecliptic System

Celestial longitude and latitude are defined with respect to the ecliptic poles. Celestial longitude is measured eastward from the ascending intersection of the ecliptic with the equator, a position known as the "first point of Aries" and place of the Sun at the time of the vernal equinox around March 21. The first point of Aries is symbolized by the ram's horns. Unlike the celestial equator, the ecliptic is fixed among the stars; however, the ecliptic longitude of a given star increases by 1.396° per century owing to the processional movement of a child's top - which shifts the first points of Aries. The first 30° along the ecliptic is nominally designated as the sign Aries, although this part of the ecliptic has now moved forward into the constellation Pisces.

MANIFESTATION OF THE UNIVERSAL FLAG
Chapter 14

The universal flag of the 5% cycle consists of the sun 7 moon and stars. This formation shows the universal state of being symbolic to, man, woman, child and the Universe. The seven represents God or man and the sun. It stands in a position to show man catering the womb or equality of the woman (moon). The star represents the understanding of man and the woman's unity the child. The five points of the star shows that it possesses Gods wisdom giving it the power of 9 also elevating it to the supreme guidance of the universe. When you add seven to the five points on the star, you will see knowledge wisdom.

You add on the two points of the moon (wisdom) and you will see Gods wisdom being born to knowledge the culture, which advocates truth and righteousness in the nation, for within truth is a wise man and his cipher, this is why the star is also the understanding seed (child) and has five points. The 8 points on the flag represents the universal builders and within each point you have a light side and dark side, this only tells of the original 16 shades of black, eight shades of brown, and eight shades of yellow. You have four long points and four short points. The distance from the long to short points, equals 45 degrees (8 x 45 = 360) showing that the flag is complete. The distance between the long points equals 90 degrees (4 x 90 = 360) this is the completion of life. The 22 points on the flag shows victory or wisdom within wisdom or the culture I God. (Peace to the NGE)

ASIATIC CONSTITUTION
Chapter 15

The Culture Is I-God
Past Masters Key

A Free Asiatic National and International Constitution for Free Asiatics, the Constitution for the Asiatic Nation of North America, referred to as Negro, Colored, Black, African, Indian, West Indian and Caribbean by Europeans the world over. This Constitution is the foundation of 'The Book: The Culture Is I-God, 1 & 2'.

Article I
Twelve Signs

The Twelve signs of the Zodiac and the Code of Supreme Mathematics scaling from one to nine and then the cipher, and the seven sciences, comprise, The Constitution of the living Asiatic Nation of North America referred to as; 'Negroes' who ruled the Universe, the oceans of the earth and the Twelve signs of the Zodiac before the separation of the Earth and Moon, up and until the Amazon Dutch German, Catholic Priesthood Fathers of the Revolution of 1789, and the Sisterhood of the Magna Charta, also the Emancipation

Proclamation, and the Union Society of European Supremacy in the year of 1863 (BCE), won the Americas in a war.

The twelve Jurymen of the fifty Union States Society and the nine Judges of the Supreme Court were founded upon the Asiatic Nation. Thus, without the Asiatic Nation the Magna Charta, Emancipation Proclamation and the Union Society's myth of European Supremacy, could not have been founded in 1863. The Magna Charta granted freedom to the blonde masses. The Emancipation Proclamation reiterated the Slaves as property. The Municipal Civil Law Code of the United States is an incorporated political unit set up by each State of the Union based on the Roman law, England Codes, Spain culture and the Lodges of France.

Article II
Birth Rites of All Asiatics

The Magna Charta granted freedom to the European masses. The Emancipation Proclamation reiterated the Slaves as property. The Municipal Civil Law Code of the United States is an incorporated political unit set up by each State of the Union based on the Rome, France and England.

Since the twelve Juryman's of the fifty Union States, Magna Charta and their document of European - American Supremacy, and the nine Judges of their Supreme Court were founded upon the Zodiac with Twelve signs and 1-9 plus 0 Supreme Numbers, then, the Lawmakers do not have any jurisdiction over any of the Free Asiatics in the inherited land of the United States of America, Canada, Central and South America etc. The Magna Carta, Civil Law Code, governs the rights and conduct of the Europeans and European-Americans.

The Free Asiatic Nationality and their Titles and/or Family names: Shabazz, El, Dey, Bey, Allah, Ali and Al etc, are their inherited title and or last name, without legal due process of the Lawmakers (Rule-makers) of the Union Society, because what our Fore Fathers were, we are that today without a contradiction. This planet is the inherited home of all Earthlings.

Article III
Taxes and Military Exemption

The Asiatics, referred to as Negroes; can never, become members and citizens of the Union Society of the fifty States. Therefore, they cannot be forced or drafted into the Unions, Army or Military service to fight for the Magna Charta, and its code of European—American supremacy.

The Rule-makers of the 50 States Union Order, cannot force the Asiatics to pay taxes, because taxation without representation is a supreme violation of the Unions Constitution. The Union Lawmakers (Rule-makers), should denounce their immoral Magna Charta Code and resort to the Constitution for the United States.

The Asiatics should not be compelled to pay labor taxes, because not everyone in the Union Society should be tax on their labor by the Rule-makers of the US government. The Asiatic Nation does not have any room for ignorance, crime, drugs, slavery, race, color, war or injustice.

Article IV
Adequate Employment and Protection

Every Lawmaker and the heads of industry and business enterprises of the 50 States Union Order are obligated members and citizens of the Magna Charta, Christian Church and Temple system of Christ, King of the Jews, meaning Jury over the wealth and freedom of the true and living Asiatic Nation of North America. Therefore, by the Asiatic Constitution, the names; **Ali, Bey, El, Dey, Al, Shabazz** and **Allah** etc., can create adequate employment, food, clothing, shelter, love, peace and happiness. The Asiatics, will and must demand respect for women and children.

The Asiatic man must and will protect the children from mob violence, rape and injustices, without being obligated to the Union Church and Religions system of the Order of Christ, the European-American Father, Son, and Holy Ghost. Truth needs no doctrine because it is supreme. Money does not make a man; it is free national standards and power that makes a man and a Nation.

Article V
Marriage License Code and the Universal Law of Nature

Truth cannot be altered and therefore it does not need an apology, neither God's doctrine, because it is supreme thought for the entire Asiatic Family, man woman and child, all those who claim their National descent names; shall be free Asiatics the world over.

The Brotherhood of Christian sons made up the marriage laws founded on the teachings of the church fathers of the Roman Catholic Priesthood. Thus, the Sisterhood Christian Daughters of the American Revolution (DAR) also help established the marriage license, States rights and codes.
Man and woman are married by the supreme law of nature. A marriage license is in violation of the laws of nature. The union between man and woman spells love with the reproduction of a child, which a marriage license, plays no part in.

The Pope, Priest, Preacher and Judges of the Christian Society know that Adam (A'su) and Eve (We-it) did not have a marriage license, the marriage licenses, does not belong to the teachings of Jesus. The marriage license code is an act of selling man and woman to one another. This is what the European-American has done to his woman and by doing, this has made her and him a slave to the State. The marriage laws came from the Roman Nations of whom crucified Jesus of Nazareth (Matthew 27:27), Ihshvh (Yeheshua) the Savior symbolize by the pentagram on the cross. Preachers, money, license, nor Religions, are needed in the marriage rules of the world.

There are not any illegitimate children that can come from woman, who is the gate of creation of both male and female children by the laws of nature. Man is the creator of both male and female children through his seed, IHVH is the Grand Architecture of the Asiatic family. A'su (Adam) means, the positive and negative forces in the son of man, and We-it (Eve) means the neutral forces of woman and daughters, responsible for a nation under reproduction of children.

People born under the opposite signs and the angle signs are in harmony with one another in ever manner. First hand knowledge of the sign under which you and your mate were born, will guide your destiny in Love, Peace and Happiness, this is not a theory. Man and Woman will know their duty toward each other and their children without being forced by the traditional code of the courtroom.

The Union Magna Charta marriage license code caused the woman and man to be cut off from the family of the Universe. The women of this world were social slave against their will and desire. A preacher, money license or religion is not necessary in the standard marriage law. The Zodiac is the standard for marriage and Asiatic guidance. By not following this law can cause the people to carry in their brains a secret sorrow and anger which causes their children to inherit a tendency of crime, hatred, insanity and various other diseases. The Twelve Jewels or Zodiac Marriage Laws can free Man and Woman. The elements of the signs are man and woman, the opposite signs are man and woman and the first marriage came from the Zodiac.

Fire—Aries and Libra—Air
Earth—Taurus and Scorpio—Water
Air—Gemini and Sagittarius—Fire
Water—Cancer and Capricorn—Earth
Fire—Leo and Aquarius—Air
Earth—Virgo and Pisces—Water
(Natural Birth Order)

The keystone is one twelfth of the circle, one sign of the Zodiac. The four fixed signs of the Zodiac form the square of matter or the four material bodies of man. The three fiery signs of the Zodiac form the three spiritual bodies of man.
The seven signs of the Zodiac demonstrate the seven fold man. The three spiritual bodies imprisoned in their four material tombs. The three signs, Cancer, Leo and Virgo, are feminine, the four signs Libra, Scorpio, Sagittarius and Capricorn are masculine. The five un-manifested signs represent the Royal Arch.

Article VI
Asiatics

The Asiatics of North America are descendants of the Ancient Canaanites, Moabites, Hamites, Cushites, Shemites, Japhethites, Chalideans and the Magis of Egypt. The Free Asiatics are guided by the laws of the Universe. The European—American is guided by the Magna Charta traditions and customs. The Christian Law system is a rule of actions recorded on paper and supported by force in the form of Protocols. The Laws of the Original Nation are recorded in nature as knowledge of the Sun, Seven, Moon, Star and Comets; this will prevent the Asiatics from indulging in crime, then we as Asiatics will not have to appear in court to stand trial. Free Asiatics do not indulge in criminal acts such as Cocaine, Robbery, Violence, and Sodomy, Deadly-Force, Forgery, Prostitution, Illegal Schemes or breaking peace in any form.

Asiatics should not remove their Fez, Turbin, or equivalent etc, from their head in any courtroom in the Union Society. This Constitution, card and book do not protect criminals. Beware!

The 1863 Bible Story of Adam and Eve were founded upon the twelve signs of Law, Positive and Negative forces of Nature, also male and female ciphers of life. The European—American, his customs and traditions, must be respected by all the Asiatic Nations, without submitting to the Magna Charta. The Asiatics land extends from Alaska to Chile. In favor of Justice: Learn the Laws of the Universe.

The Asiatic (Black) Nation gives honor to Marcus Garvey, Noble Drew Ali, WF Muhummed, Elijah Muhummed and Father Allah, the five on the right, C. Kirkman Bey and C.M. Bey, the two on the left.

Article VII
Legal Rights of Free Asiatics

The Asiatics cannot be forced to take an oath over the Bible. The Asiatics should not employ unconscious Lawyers to represent them, Europeans and their unconscious 'Negros' can never represent a Free Asiatic. The 'Negro' is the property of the Union Society slaveholders.

The Asiatics must respect the court room by saying: 'I affirm that I will keep all part or parts of Constitutional Law, which I have received as an Asiatic, also let it be recorded that this Union court does not have jurisdiction over a Free Asiatic'. This makes you qualified to be defend by the Constitution for the United States of America.

The Dutch Anglo Priest Church Fathers overthrew the last strong hold of the Moors between 1700 and 1865, this is why the Asiatic Constitution will conflict with the Priesthood Christian Union customs and creed. The Asiatic Constitution is for the Man, woman and child and the Magna Charta of 1854 is for the European—American. The European—American who are the founders of the Union Society will attempt to ignore the Asiatic Constitution and the birth rights of the Asiatics, until we come together, As One. The names, religions, and churches, were established by the Dutch Anglo Saxon Priesthood Franciscan of Europe who overthrew the Asiatic Society between 1789, and the Union of 1863.

An Asiatic, must never attempt to teach or lecture in the Christian Institutions, it is a violation of the Magna Charta code of Mary and Christ, for the Union States. Do not criticize the European—Americans belief in the religion of their son and woman image. The "Magna Carta"; is a Latin phrase meaning Magnate Charter of European economic and social attraction, which had its beginning in the colonies of New Amsterdam, Pennsylvania, Ohio, Michigan, Indiana and Illinois in 1848, thru 1854.

The Culture Is I-God Your Masters Key of Civilization (Divine Understanding Born Allah Copy Righted 1991 ace) All Rights Reserved for All Free Asiatic Amexem people. This is the Asiatic Constitution for the Asiatic Nation of North America, referred to as; Negro, African, Indian, West Indian and colored people, and White people and Jews. Ones reproduction of this Constitution is subject to a penalty. **This Constitution is the foundation of my copyrighted Book: The Culture Is I-God, Book I and II.**

If the lawmakers of the 50 union states of North America. Should attempt to ignore the Asiatic Amexem Constitutional Law and birthrights of this document. It would be an act of supreme violation of the Magna Charta Code.

FREEMAN/NISA
Chapter 16

We are self-conscious now, because we are slaves breaking from slavery. We destroy slavery in the world, and in our minds. We see it in our brains as evil, as the devil collecting and using our energies to pervert the world. We cannot pause, only action, which is divine. Words are wonderful, but deeds are divine.

We talk about man and woman as if we are separate because we have been separated, our hands reach out for each other, for the closeness, the completeness we are for each other, the expansion of consciousness that we provide for each other. We were separated by the deed and process of slavery. We internalized the process, permitting it to create an alien geography in our skulls, a wandering of prana that had us missing each other, and never understanding just what it was. After we were gone from each other; my hand might rest on yours, and still you would be gone; and I, of course, not there, out wandering, among the rogues and whores of the universe.

Therefore, this separation is the cause of our need for self-consciousness, and eventual healing. However, we must erase the separateness by providing ourselves with healthy Asiatic identities. By embracing, a value system that knows of no separation but only of the divine complement the Asiatic woman is for her man.

For in-stance, we do not believe in "equality" of men and women. We cannot understand what devils and the devilishly influenced mean when they say equality for women-kind. We could never be equals. Nature has not provided thus. The brother says, "Let a woman be a woman, and let a man be a man. Nevertheless, this means that we will complement each other, that you, who I call my house, because there is no house without a man and his woman, for they are the single element in the universe that perfectly complete their essence. Woman you are essential to the development of any life in the house because you are that house's completion.

When we say complement, completes, we mean that we have certain functions which are more natural to us, and you have certain graces that are yours alone. How do you inspire the Asiatic man? By being the conscious rising essence of Life, with the babies. Woman conscious of her-self, which is what we mean by cultured, Asiatic consciousness, and the Asiatic race, by identity, and by action. You inspire the Asiatic man by being the Asiatic Woman. By being the nation, as the house, the smallest example of how the nation should be. Therefore, you are my house, I live in you, together we have a home, and that must be the microcosm, by example, of the entire Asiatic nation. 'Our nation is our selves'.

What ever we are doing, is what the nation is doing or not doing is what the nation is or is not. You inspire the man by creating with him a new world. We seek this by bring in a new life that must be provided for, at all costs. By being a breath of the future as well as a living manifestation of our traditional greatness. Everything we do must be toward fashioning a new way, dedicating our selves to an Islamic value system, not 13th century Islam but that, which came with the stars and mood of the original people. The house we live in, the clothes we wear, the food we eat, the words we speak, must reinforce our move for National Liberation and the new consciousness of the million year old personality, and it is the woman who must reinforce these thrusts in the babies. She is the creator of the environment. The need to expand this environment, to control our space, so that we will be able to create a complementary, beneficial environment for Asiatic people and a new world consciousness is the path of National Liberation, Inspire, to raise the spirit of, to constantly lift us to what we have to do. To inspire is to be the new consciousness, so that we must be defenders and developers of this new consciousness. You must be what we need, to survive, the strength, the health, the dignity, which is this new, millennia's raging beauty. To inspire, is to be consciousness, and this act alone is teaching. To teach the children this new consciousness, to give them a value for liberation, for National Liberation, To teach them to keep their spirits free of the alien value system: to shape them in the master teachings of the Asiatic National the new national order called AOFA, the doctrine of the (5) on the left and the (2) on the right. Education is the root of development it is also defense. When we speak of Asiatic Power we mean, self-respect, self-determination and self-defense. (Wing Chung)

To teach the children, to educate the children, is to make our future predictable, and positive. Our children are our future. Who controls your life even after the body has fell we must make sure our children are Asiatic not Black, Colored, Negro and any other name that the devil gave us, not only by culture but through power of consciousness. Education is the development of consciousness, Asiatic consciousness.

If the brothers are to fly in the face of, and confront, finally, to defeat, evil, our sisters, in that same struggle, must know the reasons we are struggling, and they must continue to teach, even if we are gone, weather our absence is temporary or permanent. It must be Asiatic consciousness that is given to our babies with their milk, and with the warmth of the Asiatic woman's loving body. Asiatic consciousness, survival training, inspiration it must be their natural heritage, and earliest environmental vibration, provided for, and emphasized by our women.

Our women will and shall organize the original free school in their womb. In addition, the God Father Allah has organized the **NGE** here in North America named after the original man in North West Amexem. It is to project our children in our own image. From 1 thru 9 they are taught, then the cipher, this is Allah; all praises to the original man. They are taught who they are, what they are, and what they must grow up to do. What is provided is identity and purpose and direction, an Islamic value system taught by Father Allah; the mothers of the Nation must be the earliest examples they are conscious of the future original nation composed of children. Who is in control of their minds? Each day many Asiatic people send their children to school for 6 hours a day 5 days a week to learn European ideology.

Finally at the end of this training they learn, and many submit, and become European ideologists them selves. It is Asiatic Fathers who must teach Asiatic Mothers, and Asiatic Families who must teach American Mothers, and American Families, it is the original women, who are from the earliest living memory closest, therefore, of perhaps deepest value at teaching the sisters. Mothers must have Inspiration, to provide us with energy to reshape the world, to teach the children, so that they will understand, and take up the talk with their children in the future.

When we say social development, we are talking about the living together as a community, the communing of the community, and how that is manifested. How do we have life together, and is it beneficial? The community itself is intelligence, it is a living entity, shaped by and shaping its external environment. Nevertheless, by what internal laws do we cohere, as a people? By what organic laws of consciousness, that we actually subscribe to, actually live according to, by what real laws do we arrange our-selves in awe of, in response to. Despite, but even so, because of, and in spite of, the devil, we are organized among ourselves as a people. A free people have organizations, not necessarily in the actual framework of the colonizers program, but developed in an Islamic measure because of the light we possess, we are Free Asiatics; we have relationships with each other that exist exclusively because of the lectio.

The arc of our conscious expansion is infinity, because we can grow in absolute openness to express the magi of our 78 trillion year experience in this Universe. We are Supreme Mathematics in our world, in varying degrees, to different ends, for different reasons, depending on where we are in the Great God of the universe's mathematical framework, and we have a community. For some it is a memory, a melody, a jiggling of their leg, a way up in "life." We have a nation. Our men are men. Our women are our women. The smoke filled miniature cosmic toilet is the Union Society. That is why we cannot always see each other. That is why we cannot always really be in tune. However, we as Gods and Earths have the culture and freedom of organization and nationhood and an actual Islamic structure now, as a nation, a nation in truth.

We are saying that we have an indestructible structure, rite and reason, memory and fact. Our life style will be wisdom, power and beauty with no interference. The resistance we turn into light and heat. The liberating consciousness will consciously evolved, consciously developed, and be created stronger with 120. The woman must encourage the seeds of freedom in her every act. Social Development means education, health, the home, the community and how it relates to the Free Asiatics, how they can be drawn into it as contributors of their own consciousness evolving into what you call politicize, nationalize and socialize. What is a nationalist lifestyle and ethnos? Sisters you in your dealing with the creative degrees, to be submissive to 120, to envelope intelligence, is necessary to re-create this world pattern by an act of the will of the people. We are fighting a war, yes, but the most crucial part of that war now is the developing of the army's consciousness. To give them the will, hence the time, to resist & survive, and finally to make change. To exist to survive, to develop a value for recreating the political intelligence of the nation, social development means to advocate a society or company of persons for one common purpose.

We will evolve from the life style of a conquered, colonized, people, to that of Gods and Earths. Every breath must be prana, every step on the square. Women learn the priorities of nation building, and be an example of why we want a nation, in the first place.

Nevertheless, you must complement us, so we are whole. What we do, all our energy, is to be the male part of a free people. All that love and faith must be the connector, as a national purpose, of the original woman to the original man that answers a living creation called nation. The Europeans have reintroduced womankind precise purpose of stunting the nation, and changing the young Asiatic would be Nationals into a snarling attachment of a political power that is not for our people. Must it be our fate to be the police dogs of "Revolutionary Europeans," egged on by Sheena, 'Tarzan's spare part'.

Asiatic woman understand that there is no future for the Asiatic nation addicted to the integrated political consciousness! That is just the newest order of European rule. As another group, we shuffle to the music of another jargon, another reason, for being with the oppressor's man or woman. A nation is a whole people, the Asiatic woman must be the one-half and the Asiatic man must be the other half of our life sign, our eternal manifestation. This has to be easy to understand.
As long as any thing separates the Asiatic man and the Asiatic woman from moving together, being together, being absolutely in tune, each doing what they are supposed to do, then the nation will never re-emerge. Our first step must be to understand that we simply are different aspects of a single being.

Asiatic Literature

Men need a pattern for their lives they love to follow not to lead; this book was given to the Free Asiatics in the year, 15077/Aquarius/24/ AC...

Those Asiatics who fail to recognize the free national name of their constitutional government are classed as undesirables and are subject to all inferior names, abuses and mistreatment that the citizens care to bestow upon them. It is a sin for my people to cling to the names and the principles that delude to slavery and not to the constitutional laws of a free national government. The Great God Allah has prepared this order, to warn the people to go back to the state of mind of their Ancestors Divine and national principles so that they will be law abiders and receive their Divine right as citizens, according to the Free Asiatic Constitution that was prepared for all Free Asiatics. The Asiatics are to claim their own free national name and creed. There is but, one issue for them to be recognized by this government and the governments of the earth, and it comes through the Free Asiatic Movement, which is incorporated in this government. Through it, they and their children can receive their Divine rights, unmolested by other citizens, so that they can cast a free national ballot at the polls under the government and not under a granted privilege, as has been the existing condition for many generations.

You who doubt whether the principles of the Asiatic Nation are right for the redemption of the Asiatic people, go to those that know law in City Hall and among the officials in your government and ask them under an intelligent tone, and they will be glad to render you a favorable reply, for they are glad to see this order bring you out of darkness into marvelous light. Money does not make the man, free national standards and power make a man and nation. The wealth of all national governments, gold, silver and commerce, belong to the citizens alone and without your national citizenship by name and principle, you have no true wealth. We as Asiatic Naturals are calling on all true Asiatics that stand for a Natural Free Government and the enforcement of the Constitution to help the so-called Black people because they need all the support from all the true Asiatics who are to be citizens of the North Gate also known as North West Amexem (North America). Help us, as Asiatics, to save our people who have fallen from the constitutional laws. We are depending on your support to get them back to the constitutional fold again, so that they will learn to love instead of hate and will live according to Love, Truth, Peace, Freedom and Justice supporting a free national constitution of the united Asiatics in America.

We, as Asiatics, love our people and desire their unity back to their own free National and Divine standard because day by day they have been violating the national and constitutional laws by claiming names and principles that are unconstitutional.
If Japanese, Chinese, Greeks, Italians, Arabians, Turks, etc., are forced to proclaim their free national name and creed before the constitutional government of the US, it is no more than right that the law should be enforced upon all other American citizens alike. In all other governments when a man or woman is born, raised, and asked for his national descent name and he or her fails to give it, he or her is misused, imprisoned or exiled. Any group of people that fails to answer to the constitutional standards of law by name and principles are not free because to be a citizen of any government, you must claim your national descent name.

The word 'negro' deludes in the Latin language to the word 'nigger'. The same as the word 'colored' deludes to anything that is painted, varnished or dyed. Every nation must bear a national descent name of their ancestors because by honoring thy father and thy mother, your days will he lengthened upon this earth. These names such as Smith, Poole, Dixon,

Johnson, Richard etc, have never been recognized by any US citizen of this day for so-called Black people. Through your free national name, you are known and recognized by all nations of the earth that are recognized by the said national government in which they live.

The 14th and 15th Amendments brought the North and South in unit, placing the Southerners, who were at that time without power, with the constitutional body of power. At that time, (1865) the free national constitutional law that was enforced in 1774 by the US declared all men equal and free'.

If all men are declared by the free national constitution to be free and equal, (since that constitution has never been changed), 'there is no need for the application of the 14th and 15th Amendments for the salvation of our people as citizens. There is not but one Supreme issue for our people to use to redeem that which was lost, and that is through the above statements (supra). If the citizens and our people in this government do not carry out the above principles, the worst is yet to come. In the words of the Noble Drew All, 'The Great God of the Universe is not pleased with the works that are being performed in North America, and this great sin must be removed from the land to save it from enormous earthquakes, diseases, etc'. The Gods & Earths know and understand that 120 lessons are preparing this generation of the Asiatics to help our people. The Gods truly know that our people will find the true and divine way of their Ancestors and learn to stop serving carnal customs and merely ideas of humankind that have never done them any good, but have always harmed them. The Asiatics, without understanding, have fallen from the true light into utter darkness of sin. There is not a nation on earth today that will recognize them socially, religiously, politically or economically in their present condition of their endeavor in which they themselves try to force upon a world that their ancestors civilized, they will not refrain from their sinful ways of action, and their deeds have brought death, drugs and everything that brings harm to beings of the Asiatic (Black) race on earth. They fought the Southerner for the US, but if you travel in the North, South, East and West, and examine conditions there, you will see it is the works of our people continuously practicing the things, which bring dishonor, disgrace and disrespect to any nation that lives the life of my people running after the God of Humankind.
We, as Asiatics, are calling on all true citizens of the Americas for moral support to help us in our great work of bringing our people out of darkness and into marvelous light. Our Divine and National movement stands for the specific Grand principles of Love, Truth, Peace, Freedom and Justice.

With the origin of the millions of people in this country who can trace their ancestors back to the illustrious founders of civilization, we will remind the descendants of these people of the time when their forefathers were the main people to spread the most progressive ideas of civilization. In fact, they saved civilization many times, when barbaric tribes from Europe were ravishing all Countries, which they were permitted to enter. It was the ancestors of the Asiatic Nations that saved the historic records when the burning of libraries was a fad.

Asiatics are Moabites, Hamathites and Canaanites etc, who were driven out of the land of Canaan and received permission from their Brother the Pharoh of Kamit to settle in a portion of Kamit. In later years, each tribe formed kingdoms. These kingdoms are now called Alkebulan, Morocco, Algiers, Tunis, Tripoli, Spain, England and America.

Inspired by the lofty teachings of the 120 degrees, we have it as the revealed word. We shall foster the principles of its teachings among our nation. We must promote economic security. The preaching of economic security among us is by no means as widespread and intensive as the circumstances demand.

No other thing is needed more among us at this time than greater economic power. Better positions for our men and women, more business employment for our boys and girls and bigger incomes will follow our economic security. We shall be secure in nothing until we have economic power.

A beggar people cannot develop the highest in them, nor can they attain to a genuine enjoyment of the spirituality of life. Our men, women and children will be taught to succeed in a group capacity in business, in spite of the trials and failures of some of them. Trials and failures in business are by no means confined to any particular group of people. Some business ventures of all people fail. We have many men and women among our people who are qualified, both by training and experience, who are shining lights in the business world. Our business enterprises in every field of endeavor should have the fullest confidence, cooperation and patronage of all Asiatics whenever and wherever they can be given.

Neophyte Questions For Free Asiatics

1. Who created you? Allah.
2. Who is Allah? Allah is the Master Architect.
3. Can we see Him? Yes. The all-seeing eye; third eye (Man).
4. What is a Prophet? A Prophet is a thought of Allah manifested in the flesh.
5. What does Noble Drew Ali born? 120 degrees. (Add-up each letter in his name)
6. Where is the quiet, quiet voice? In the MIND.
7. What is the duty of an Asiatic? To teach knowledge, wisdom, understanding.
8. Who is the founder of LIGHT? Allah.
9. What year was the NGE founded? 1964.
10. Where? The North Gate (Mecca) NYC.
11. Where was the original man born? In the MIND.
12. What is your nationality? Asiatic.
13. What is your race? The pale person is in a race with time.
14. Why are we Asiatic? Because we are descendants of Gods born on Earth.
15. For what purpose was, the NGE founded? For the uplifting and teaching of the fallen Asiatic Nation.
16. What is our religion? The original man submits to no religion.
17. What is our culture/creed? I-God.
18. How old is the Original man? Older than the Sun, Moon and Stars.
19. Do we fly a banner or flag? A flag.

20. What is our sign and symbol? The Sun, seven, Moon and Star.
21. Which is our Holy Day? Friday.
22. Why? Because Friday is the 7th day in the Asiatic Calendar.
23. Who is Ruth? Ruth is an Asiatic woman.
24. What is the name man? Allah.
25. Where was the Asiatic Empire? Earth.
26. What is the modern name for Amexem? Earth/Asia.
27. What does the name Jesus mean? Justice.
28. How long is the river Nile? 4,690 miles long.
29. What are Angels used for? To carry messages to the four corners of the world.
30. Where did Jesus teach? Asia-minor, Europe and India.
31. What is TRUTH? Aught.
32. What is AUGHT? Allah.
33. Where was the moon 66 trillion years ago? In the Pacific Ocean.
34. Where is the Garden of Eden? The Asiatic women.
35. Where is Canaan? North Amexem.
36. What is the name for the Garden of Eden? Wisdom/Equality.
37. Are Adam and Eve your Father and Mother? Emphatically, No!
38. Are you human? No! For I am the Original Man who is God!
39. Can an Asiatic be humankind? No!
40. What are the modern names for the Angels? Asiatics Blackman, Woman and Child.
41. What is the shade of their skin? Olive (ripen).
42. Are the Asiatics any relation to those Angels? Yes, we have the same Father and Mother.
43. How many selves are there? 2 a higher and lower.
44. Who represents the higher self? Angels, Asiatics, God Allah.
45. What person represents the lower self? Those we ran out of the Holy City and those who teach their teachings.
46. Can the higher self pass away? No!
47. Why? Because that is Allah who is Man.
48. What is the lower self? Hatred, Slander, Lewdness, Theft and Murder.
49. Who is the European? He is a shadow of our lower self.
50. Who is Muhammed of Mecca? A Prophet of Allah.
51. What is Byzantine? See 1453 AD.
52. What does the European call us? Negro, Black, Colored and Ethiopian.
53. Are you Black? See the First Degree in the 1-10.
54. Why? See the First Degree in the 1-40.
55. Why? Because man is Allah.
56. What does Ethiopia mean? Divided and or burnt face people, and that name was given to us by the Greeks.
57. Will you define the word Colored. See the 2nd degree in the 1-10.
58. Who was King David? The son of Jesse.
59. Who was Solomon? An Asiatic King.
59. Who is your Father? Allah.
60. When will we be as one? When we as Asiatics come together as one (One=3+4=7).
61. Is the Devil made or created? Made.

62. How many degrees do you have? 360 degrees.
63. Tell me about Elohim? See Gematria.
64. Who is Jesse? The son of Obed.
65. Who is Obed? The son of Boaz, of the tribe of Judah.

Advance Questions
for Neophytes

1. Why are you wearing that emblem? I was raised to wear it.
2. I see you are a traveling man (Asiatic), do you travel alone? No good man (Asiatic) ever travels alone.
3. You are a carpenter, I see? Yes, I am building a spiritual Temple.
4. What country is your mother from? She is from the tribe of Moab/Shabazz or the God Tribe.
5. Have you ever had your shoes off? Yes, I was barefoot when I was in the Holy of Holies.
6. You look like you might have a Pot of Incense? I have a grateful heart.
7. An initiatory ceremony is symbolic of what? A mystical rebirth.
8. What pieces of furniture do you have in your house? The Bible, Qur'an, Compasses, Square and Charter.
9. How are the lights placed in your house? Lights are in the East, West, and South, but the Star is in the North.
10. What seaport was the timber for the temple brought from? Joppa.
11. What is a quadrant? The 4th part of the circumference of a circle.
12. How many pillars did you encounter as Asiatic? Seven.
13. What did the Higher-self say to the Lower-self at one time when He met Him? Where are you going Satan?
14. What was the answer that the Lower-self gave to the Higher-self? 'I am going to and fro the earth seeking whom I may devour'.
15. When was the legend Hiram Abiff introduced into Speculative Masonry? Between 1723 to 1729, more likely 1725.
16. Who took the light from Africa into Europe? The Moors who are Asiatic.
17. Who dealt the worst form of slavery ever recorded in human history? England, France and America.
18. Who is Set? One of the members of the company of the Gods of Annu.
19. Who is Nu? Father of the Gods and begetter of the great company of the Gods, and Nut is the female principle of Nu (His Wisdom).
20. The Question is Meat? It is thought to be safer to eat animals that eat vegetables rather than to eat animals that eat animals.
21. What about the swine, pig and pork? The hogs are labeled as highly unsafe and unclean to eat. Worms found in hogs are difficult to destroy. In general, all animal corpses are contaminated and bacteria infested.
22. What about cooked flesh? This speeds up the putrefaction process. It is the putrefied, decayed flesh, blood, waste and pus, which gives meat its delicious taste.
23. Does adrenaline poison the flesh? Animals secrete adrenaline into their bodies as a reaction to the fear caused by the slaughterhouse.

24. Why did ALLAH send Muhummed to Arabia? To save all men, women and children of Earth.

25. What happened on Mount Zion? Solomon built his temple, King David sang his psalms; Jesus of Nazareth walked and Muhummed was wafted one night by the Archangel Gabriel that he might ascend from there to visit paradise.

26. What does Abyssinia mean? Immeasurable depth of your inner self. A former name of Ethiopia.

Fez

The Fez is a derivation of the base of the Aaku-t Khufu. Three hundred and sixty degrees is a circle; the circle has no beginning nor ending. It is infinite; it is the sign of perfection. The Fez is the perfect headdress. The dimension and geometry of the Fez are perfect mathematics. When we born Supreme Mathematics, we know that the Aaku-t Khufu are perfect structures. The Aaku-t Khufu is symbolic of the Temple of perfected man a temple that can never be destroyed. All the answers are within SELF. The Fez is the universal crown of knowledge, wisdom and understanding and is internationally recognized as such. The Fez contains a world of significant symbolism for those who understand and are conscious of what it represents. The history of this majestic crown starts with it originally being white. The oppressive powers put the Asiatics into a pit of lions, unless they would denounced the first true and divine creed for the redemption of the Asiatics, which is Islam. The lions ripped them apart because they had been eating the flesh of the animals.

The only thing left of the Asiatics was the fez, stained with blood, from that day on the Moors used the White, Red and Black Fez or as it was called in those days the Hi-Rom. The top of the fez is flat. It stands for the uncompleted portion of the Pyramid (Aaku-t Khufu). The tassel represents the cable used to raise the capstones on top of the Aaku-t Khufu, or it may also represent the imperial potentate who is assigned to finish the job. The shade of the tassel signifies the unseen reason why the job was left unfinished.

Under the head of the wearer is the vault where the treasures of the science are preserved. The red fez represents the skill and wisdom of the man who erected the Pyramid (Aaku-t Khufu). The black fez represents the chief protectors of the jewels and treasures inside the pyramid. Equally important, the fez is symbolic of the halo. It is the same halo that lingers above the Cheribums' and Seraphim' head. The fez is the official headdress of the men in the Asiatic Nation. The history of the turban can be found in Joshua Chapter 2 and Judges Chapter 13 and 17. Such is the significance of King Solomon's crown; the Fez indicated that as Master of the Temple he is the 'anointed one'.

Read the doctrines of the Five Percent Nation carefully, they contain our hopes, aims, rules and articles of life and creed, every God and Earth should have a copy of 120 lessons. In conclusion, I urge you to remember there is work enough for all to do in helping to build a better world. The problems of life are mainly social and economic in a profound sense they are moral. Look for the best in others and give them the best that is in you, have a deeper appreciation for womanhood. Brighten the hopes of our youth in order that their courage shall be increased to dare and do wondrous things. Adhere at all times to the principles of your 12 Jewels. As Asiatics, be affectionate leaders and continue to labor, day and night, both in public and in private, for your nation and help uplift the fallen men and women of the world.

God & Earth

The Gods and Earths are essentially a group of Asiatic men and women who explore and understand the universe. God and Earth seek harmony in their environment and in self. God and Earth are devoted to learning and applying such measures, which will insure a rapport between themselves and the elements of their environment, thus, they direct their thoughts and attention to every possible avenue of information and experience, nourished by knowledge, they set out to correct and amend their course in life to the betterment of themselves and all with whom they come in contact.

Such a course is the most satisfying and enduring. Knowledge cannot help but improve one's appreciation and mastery of life. However, such a course is also beset with many challenges and hurdles, which often seem insurmountable. The inherent frailties of man the jealousy, lust, indolence, and greed about him are forces that act as shackles to his desire to know and master life. For each man and woman in history who has tried to explore new frontiers, there were multitudes crying out against them. People dislike dealing with the unknown. Man must explore and know the innermost natures of life and in this pursuit of knowledge upsets are bound to occur. As new light is thrown into existing beliefs and practices, man is often obliged to change his views. Self, which is you, is subject to impressions from many more sources than those that arise from the external world of matter. It is true that all of these elements are part of you and your existence. Animate, living things, including man, have an aura. Fields of radiation, of energy, which extends around the body it can be perceived by other beings and by animals, its forces, are invisible, but they exist.

Man is a generator, he generates energies within himself. Some, such as nerve energy, have common, measurable electrical qualities. Others are of such a high frequency that their physical properties can be determined only by their effects upon persons and things. There may be a sudden emotional attraction toward the other or there may be an equally strange feeling of dislike or discomfit. Auras can and do affect inanimate objects and these, in turn, in a subtle way, affect our own auras to cause within an emotional reaction to them, if the aura is of that kind. Notice the emotional sensations you experience among strangers, in a conveyance, perhaps going to or from work; the same things work with books or magazines that obviously have been handled by many people.

Thoughts can be transferred from one mind to another; this is personal magnetism. Thought is energy; it can be transmitted under certain conditions. An experiment is to begin to concentrate upon someone, without letting the person see that you are looking in their direction, fix the whole of your attention upon them. Dismiss all other thoughts from your mind except that the person will look up in your direction, visualize this one thought, and they will look up at you.

We have two nervous systems a central and autonomic, the autonomic system is related to the central in an intricate way, the central is sight, hearing, taste, and the motor nerves. Autonomic is subliminal psychic impulses that are vibrations from a nonobjective source. Autonomic can receive subtle vibrations of energy and transfer them to the central nervous system. Here is a test to try the next time you are fatigued and need a mental stimulus, bring the thumb and the first two fingers of the right hand together, take a deep breath and gently press the fingers into the hollow at the back of the neck against the skull. Press gently, but firmly, at the same time, exhale slowly, you will feel calm, relaxed and mentally refreshed nothing more. The study of the nervous system and levels of consciousness shows how all nerve energy is electrical.

Every electrical impulse sets up an electrical or magnetic field of radiations, an electrical field surrounds a point of electrical impulses; the body is composed of a positive and negative polarities. The brain is the control board of the nervous system. Now we see by this that thoughts are thought-forms and electrical impulses. Eyes wander about receiving numerous impressions by sight with all of them being transmitted by vibrations to the brain centers where they are translated into thought-forms or pictures. Words transmitted by vibrations of an electrical nature to the nerves attached to the drums of the ears, and through the impulses received on the eardrum, send forth vibrations along the nervous system to the centers of the brain. The same is true of tasting and smelling. In ourselves, we will find not isolated powers but universal forces at work. (As above, so below) There are three universal principles or fundamental manifestations that affect the state of existence. These are called TIME, SPACE AND MIND. Space is that portion of the universe beyond the immediate influence of earth and her atmosphere. Nowhere in the universe is space empty, it is occupied by extremely tenuous matter generally gas and solids, from this we see that space and time are actually intimately intertwined. Matter exists both as gas and as dust grains in the space between stars. Space is that property of the universe associated with extension in three mutually perpendicular directions.

In the "Theory of Relativity", when the velocity of light is approached, the classical laws of gravitation no longer apply, space no longer has the relations commonly assigned to it, and time slows down, this is why time is different in space.

Our sun and the family of planets revolve around a central sun, which is millions of light years in distance, and it requires approximately 25,000 years for our sun to make one revolution in our galaxy about 2083.33 years per sign. The sun's orbit is called the zodiac which is divided into 12 signs, Aries, Taurus, Gemini, Cancer, Leo, Virgo, Libra, Scorpio, Sagittarius, Capricorn, Aquarius and Pisces, (with the earth it takes about 12 months 28 to 31 days per sign).

In conclusion, the cosmic influences are invisible, but they act upon man, heat and light are intangible and incorporeal nevertheless, they act upon man and the same is true of other invisible influences. Man's body is not the real man nor is the material universe God. Man is composed of an invisible mind and a visible body, so too God has an invisible and a visible domain, in all we say that man is God, for man is not the body nor the soul but Mind, this is why man cannot die, 'Peace From A Son of Man'.

These are the teachings of the <u>Father Allah and his 5% nation of Gods and Earths</u>. When the Father went to the streets of NYC he came with the teaching of Elijah Muhummed and WD Fard, this is what He taught the youth of America in '1964'.

The children he taught 'learned to quote these teachings' (Degrees that the "Father gave the NGE, these degrees came from temple 7 NYC under Brother Malcolm X, who was a student of Elijah Muhummed who's teacher was WD Fard, the degrees are also known as '120' and to this day, 44 years later, (2008) 'this is taught in the ghettoes of the united States of America'. Now I ask you, are we a 'Gang', 'Religious Order' or Culture?

Supreme Questions For Free Asiaitcs

1. Who created you? ALLAH
2. Who is Allah? Allah is the Father of the Universe.
3. Can we see Him? Yes!
4. Where is the nearest place we can meet Him? In the heart.
5. Who is Noble Drew Ali? He is a Prophet of Allah.
6. What is a Prophet? A Prophet is a thought of Allah manifested in the flesh.
7. What is the duty of a Prophet? To save Nations from the wrath of Allah.
8. Who are the (5) on the left and the (2) on the right? Their names are known in the Asiatic Constitution.
9. What year was the Asiatic Constitution manifested? 15077
10. Where? The North Gate.
11. Where do the (5) on the left and the (2) on the right manifest their rites? Allah.
12. What is a Nationality? That quality or character which arises from the fact of The People belonging to a Nation, especially with reference to allegiance by birth.
13. What is your Ancient Nationality? Asiatic, Moabite, Shabazz etc,.
14. What other Ancient Nationalities did we have? Ham, Cush, Canaanite, Hittite, Kamet and Kamiishen etc,.
15. Name the seven tribes of the Asiatic Nation. See the Asiatic Constitution.
16. What does Shabazz mean? 7.
17. What is your Nationality? Asiatic.
18. For what purpose are the Asiatics given Knowledge? So that they could clean up.
19. How did the circle 7 begin to uplift the Asiatics? By teaching them to know, I am.
20. What is our religion? Without being obligated to the Union Church and religious system of the Order Christ, the European Son idol god, it is a creed.
21. What is religion? Obedience and submission to mandates and precepts of a Superior Being.
22. How many Flags do the Moors have? 2.
23. What do the Flags look like? Both are red Flags, one has a five pointed green star in the center and the other has a white square on the left with a cedar tree of Lebanon in the square.

24. What do the five points on the Star represent? Love, Truth, Peace, Freedom and Justice.

25. How old are the Flags of the Moors and/or Asiatics? Over 10,000 Years Old.

26. Which day do the Moors and/or Asiatics see as a Holy day? Friday.

27. Who is IHShVH? A Prophet of Allah.

28. Why is Friday a Holy day? Because it is the 7th day.

29. How are you born? On 7 or 9.

30. Will you give in brief the line (Genealogy) through which IHShVH came. Some of the Great Fathers through which IHShVH came through are Moab, Canaan, Ham, Cush, Nahor, Ibrahim, Lot and the Neteru.

31. Why did Allah send the five on the left and the two on the right? To save the Asiatics from the iron hand oppression of the pale skin Nations of Europe and America.

32. How long has it been since the Devil was made? 6,077 years.

33. Who is Ruth's Husband? Boaz.

34. What tribe is Ruth? The Moabites, (Ruth 1:4).

35. What is the modern name for Amexem? Earth/Asia.

36. Where is the North Star? The North Gate.

37. Which way does the planet Earth rotate? East.

38. What does Jesus Born? God's Culture or Freedom.

39. Did the Angels give to the child that is raised a Holy Name? Yes; but it cannot be used by those who are slaves to sin.

40. What is the modern name for Moabite? Moor.

41. Where is the Asiatic Empire? Amexem.

42. What is an Angel? The Kundalini.

43. Where did the word Angel come from? Aggelos.

44. At what age did IHShVH teach? Knowledge Wisdom.

45. How long did he teach? Knowledge Cipher Build or Destroy.

46. What is Holy Breath? Prana.

47. At what place on Earth did the Original man land first? Mu.

48. Where is the land of Mu? Separated 66 trillion years ago by Shabazz.

49. What is the Atziloth? Emanation symbolizing the celestial realm and the element fire.

50. Name the tenth Sephiroth? (MLKVTh) Malkuth, represented by the Divine Name Adonai, (ADNI) and among the angelic hosts by the kerubim (KRVBIM).

51. Name the first Sephiroth? Kether, the Crown Exodus 3:4.

52. What is the Jetziratic world? Olahm Ha-Yetzirah, or world of formation and of angels, which proceeds from Briah, and though less refined in substance, is still without matter.

53. What is the Asiatic world? Olahm Ha-Asia, the world of action, called also the world of shells, Olahm Ha-Qliphoth, which is this world of matter.

54. Who is Samael? The angel of poison and of death, His wife is the harlot, or woman of whoredom, Isheth Zenunim; and united they are called the beast, Chioa.

55. Build on 111. (AChD HVA ALHIM) "He is One God." (ALP) Aleph, an ox, a thousand. The redeeming Bull. As the lightning lighteneth out of the East even unto the West, so shall be the coming of the Son of Man. (APL) thick darkness. AOM, the Hindu Aum or Om. (MHVLL) mad-the destruction of Reason by Illumination. (OVLH) a holocaust. **(PLA)** the Hidden Wonder, a title of Kether, (777 Qabalistic).

56. Where is Mecca for the 5%? Harlem.

57. What is the shade of the Asiatics? The shade of a Ripe Olive.

58. Give five names that are given to some of the descendants of Yacub's children! Lucifer, Satan, Devil, Dragon and Beast.

59. Tell me about the Demons. This is the grossest and most deficient of all forms (lower self).

60. What about Satan? The "shells," Qlipoth, are the demons, in whom again is a form of the Sephiroth, distorted and averse. This great dragon, which is here described, is evidently identical with the leviathan of Job. Finally, in a more exoteric sense he is Satan and the devil, the accusing one.

61. Build on the Higher self. The higher self is man clothed with soul, created in the form of Allah. The higher self is the embodiment of truth. The higher self is justice, mercy, love and right. He, who knows his higher self, knows Allah.

62. Who is W.F. Mohammed? Eleventh degree in the 1 - 40.

63. Who is the Conqueror Muhammed? 1453 AD (Byzantium Empire).

64. Name some of the marks that were put upon the Asiatics/Moors of Amexem by the European in 1774? Black, Colored, Ethiopian and Negro.

65. What is meant by the word Black? Negro!

66. What is meant by the word Negro? A member of the Black group, who originated in Africa south of the Sahara.

67. What does the word colored mean? Colored means anything that has been painted, stained, varnished or dyed.

68. What does Ethiopia mean? Something divided. (Gk) {Aithops} Ethiopian, burn, face.

69. Can a man be a Negro, Colored, Black or Ethiopian? Emphatically No!

70. Why? Because man is Allah and the womb of man is the Universe.

71. What title does Satan call Himself? God.

72. Will you define the word white? White means purity, purity means God and God is the Ruler of the land, therefore, the European cannot be White.

73. To whom do we refer to at all times as being Akbar? Allah.

74. Is the Devil God? Emphatically Now Cipher!

75. Who made the Devil? Yacub.

76 Tell us about Elohim? Plural formed from the feminine singular (ALH) Eloh, by adding IM to the word. However, in as much as IM is usually a termination of the masculine plural and is here added to a feminine noun, it gives to the word Elohim the sense of a female potency united to a masculine idea, and thereby capable of producing an offspring. The ancient of days conforms himself simultaneously into the Father and the Mother and thus begets the Son. Now this Mother is Eloh. Again, we are usually told that the Holy Spirit is masculine. Nevertheless, the word (RVCH) Ruach spirit is feminine, as appears from the following passage of the Sepher Yetzirah: (AChTh RVCh ALHIM ChIIM) Achath (feminine not Achad masculine) Ruach Elohim Chiim: One is she, the Spirit of the Elohim of life (man is YX).

Now we fine that be-fore the Deity conformed Himself thus i.e., as male and female that the worlds of the universe could not subsist, or in the words of Genesis, 'The Earth was formless and void'.

77. What is Elohim sometimes called? (Alhim=300 also ALHIM=3.14) symbol of man's will of the evil four dominated by man's Mind. Also Tetragrammaton, Yeheshua the

Savior, hence the beginning of the great work, Elohim the original mischief, but good since it is a key of the Pentagram (95=1+4=14=8+6=86).

78. How many degrees are in a circle? 360°.
79. How many days are in the circle? Seven.
80. How many days are in creation? Seven.
81. According to science, how many days are in a year? Seven.

All questions in this book were asked by an Asiatic, and answered by a Son of Father Allah, (February 7, 15077).

ZODIAC CIRCLE
Chapter 17

This orbit is called the Zodiac which is divided into 12 signs familiarly known as Aries, Taurus, Gemini, Cancer, Leo, Virgo, Libra, Scorpio (Eagle), Sagittarius, Capricorn, Aquarius and Pisces.

It requires our Solar System approximately 2,083.33 years to pass through one of these signs and this time is the measurement of an Age or Dispensation because of the precision of the Equinoxes, the movement of the cipher through the signs of the Zodiac is in order reverse from that given above.

Regarding this matter there is a disagreement among astrologers. However, from Virgo to Leo is about **2083.33** years in the Sun's orbit, the celestial precision of the equinoxes takes a total of **25,000** years to make its circuit or **2083.33** years per zodiacal sign. Therefore, the transition from Virgo to Leo was about 7 times **2,083.33** or **14,563.31** years ago, the sun traveled from Virgo to Leo. The dynastic history of Kemit starts when Taurus took over from Gemini or about **20,833.30** years ago. We are now in the cusp of the transition from Pisces to Aquarius, as of Aries/1/15086 thru Pisces/29/15186 Asiatic Calendar.

The True Trinity
1. The Aia in a perfect body
2. The Breath form in the body
3. The Aia and the Breath form in a perfect body

The three signs Cancer, Leo and Virgo are the three female signs from the breast to the womb; when squared, 3x3 they make nine. The male signs are four Libra, Scorpio, Sagittary and Capricorn from the coccyx Libra to Capricorn opposite the heart. When squared they equal 16.

Nine plus 16 equals 25. The five signs, Aquarius, Pisces, Aries, Taurus and Gemini are signs representing the hypotenuse above Cancer and Capricorn which when squared equals 25, the square of the circle thus 'squaring the circle'.

1. "Squared" the four fixed signs of the Zodiac form the four material bodies of man.
2. "Trine" the three fiery signs of the Zodiac form the three spiritual (Mental forms) bodies of man.
3. "Seven" the seven signs of the Zodiac demonstrate the sevenfold Man. The three spiritual bodies imprisoned in their material tomb.

BARNABAS
Chapter 18

Barnabas was borne in Cyprus. His name was Joses and due to the cause of Jesus, the other apostles had given him the surname of Barnabas. He continued to live as a Hebrew and practiced what Jesus had taught him. The conflict between the Jews and the followers of Jesus was started by the Jews because they felt that the Hebrews would undermine their authority. During the siege of Jerusalem in 70 AD, the followers of Jesus left the city and refused to take part in the Bar Coachaba rebellion in A D 132. With the conversion of Paul, a new period opened in European Theology. Paul's theology was based on his personal experience interpreted in the light of contemporary Greek thought. The theory of redemption was the child of his brain, a belief entirely unknown to the disciples of Jesus. Paul's theory involved the deification of Jesus.

The Pauline period in the history of the Pauline Church saw a change of scenes and principals. In place of the disciples, who had sat at the feet of Jesus, a new figure, who had not known Jesus, had come to the forefront. In place of Palestine, the Roman Empire became the scene of Pauline activity. Instead of being a mere sect of the Hebrews, Pauline-ism not only became independent of the Hebrews but also became independent of Jesus himself. Paul was a Jew and an inhabitant of Tarsus. He had spent a lot of time in Rome and was a Roman Citizen. He realizes the strong hold, which the Roman religion had on the masses. The intellectuals were under the influence of Aristotle. Because of Paul's compromise with Roman beliefs and legend, Pauline followers grew in number and grew in strength.

The followers of Barnabas never developed a central organization. Yet due to the devotion of their leaders, their numbers increased very fast. These Hebrews incurred the writhe of the Church and systematic effort was made to destroy them and to obliterate all traces of their existence including books and temples. The lesson of history, however, is that it is very difficult to destroy truth by force.

Emperor Constantine brought a greater part of Europe under his rule and secondly he began to support the Pauline's without accepting Pauline-ism. To the soldier prince the different creeds within the Jew/European and Hebrew/Asiatic were very confusing. In AD 325, a meeting of all denominations of Pauline-ism was called at Nicea (Isnik). Fearful massacre of Hebrews, who did not believe in Pauline-ism, was held, where it was ordered that all original Hebrew script should be destroyed, and in the year 325 A D, this took place at the Nicene Council.

The 12 Apostles of Jesus:
  1. Peter (Also Known As Simon Peter)
  2. Andrew (Simon Peter's Brother)
  3. James son of Zebedee
  4. John (James' Brother)
  5. Philip
  6. Bartholomew
  7. Thomas
  8. Matthew
  9. James son of Alphaeus
  10. Thaddaeus (Judas, Son of James)
  11. Simon the Zealot
  12. Judas Iscariot (Who Betrayed Jesus)
    • Matthias (Who Replaced Judas)

Paul, also known as Saul, was born in Tarsus of Cilcia in Asia Minor. His family was of the line of Benjamin. He grew up in Jerusalem and studied Jewish tradition under the elder Gamaliel, becoming a zealous Pharisee. Paul was at first an active opponent of the Christian movement. He took care of the cloaks of those who stoned Stephen (Acts 7:58, 22:20). On his way to Damascus to persecute Christian believers, he was stopped by a blinding light, and a voice that said, "Saul, Saul, why do you persecute Me?" Paul asked, "who are You Lord?" The reply came, "I am Jesus, whom you are persecuting. But get up and enter the city, and you will be told what you are to do." Paul then converted to Christianity. In addition, his zeal to persecute the early Christians was re-channeled into preaching the Gospel. Paul made three missionary journeys around Asia Minor, Macedonia and Achaia. He is the author of thirteen New Testament letters - Romans, 1 and 2 Corinthians, Galatians, Ephesians, Philippians, Colossians, 1 and 2 Thessalonians, 1 and 2 Timothy, Titus, and Philemon. He might have written to the Hebrews.
With the exception of Romans, all of Paul's letters were written to churches or individuals whom he knew personally. The focus of Paul's writings is Jesus, through whom God has affected redemption for all people regardless of ethnic or social background.
Paul was thrown into prison, whipped, stoned, punched, and shipwrecked many times, but never gave up his preaching of Christ. He might have been the most zealous and hardest working Apostle of all time. It is believed that Paul was beheaded in Rome under Nero in about AD 67.

An Age

It is conceded by all critical students that the sun entered the zodiacal sign Taurian in the days of "Adam" when the Taurian Age began, that Abraham lived not far from the age of Aries and about the time of the rise of the Roman Empire, the sun entered the sign Pisces; word is bond!

Piscean Age

The word Pisces means fish. The sign is known as a water sign, and the Piscean Age has been distinctly the age of the fish and its element water. John the Harbinger and Jesus both understood the rite of water baptism which has been used in some form in all thee so-called Christian Churches and cults, even to the present time. Fish was a symbol for Jesus, not the cross. The Asiatic people are today standing upon the cusp of the Piscean Aquarian Ages. Aquarius is an air sign and the New Age is already noted for remarkable Asiatic brothers etc. Men and Women navigate the air as fish do the sea and send their thoughts spinning around the world with the speed of light. The word Aquarius is derived from Asiatic Latin aqua, meaning water. Aquarius is however, the water bearer and the symbol of the sign, which is the 11th sign of the Zodiac is a man carrying in his right hand a pitcher of water. The transfer of dominion from one Age to another is an important event in the world of Cherubim and Seraphim. The four and twenty cherubim and Seraphim that guard the cycle of the sun, the mighty ones who were proclaimed by masters long ago the four and twenty ancient ones. Every sign in the entire Zodiac is ruled by two, a Cherubim and Seraphim. The guardian of the Piscean Age; Ramasa is the Cherubim; Vacabi El is the Seraphim. The guardian of the Aquarian Age, Archer is the Cherubim; Sakmaqu El is the Seraphim. The crown will be lifted from the head of one and put on the other of the Cherubim when the Ages change every 2,083.33 years. When the royal scepter is transferred from Seraphim, too Seraphim there will be deep silence in the courts of the universe.

Son of Man

From Allah "Time never was when man was not. If life of man at any time began, a time would come when it would end. The thoughts of Allah cannot be circumscribed. No finite brain can comprehend things infinite. All finite things are subject unto change. All finite things will cease to be because there was a time when they were not. The bodies and the souls of men are finite things and they will change, yea from the finite point of view the time will come when they will be no more. However, man himself is not the body, nor the soul, man is mind and is Allah. Creative Fiat gave to man, to the original man, a soul that he might function on the plane of soul, gave him a body of the flesh that he might function on the plane of things made manifest.

Why did creative Fiat give to the original man a soul that he might function on the plane of soul? Why did creative Fiat give to soul a body of the flesh that he might function on the plane of things that are made manifest? Hear now ye worlds, dominions, powers and thrones! Hear now ye cherubim, ye seraphim, ye angels and ye men! Hear now 0 protoplast, earth, plant, and beast! Hear now ye creeping things of earth, ye fish that swim, ye birds that fly! Hear now ye winds that blow, ye thunders and ye lighting of the sky! Hear now ye vibrations of the fire, of water, earth and air! Hear now O, every thing that is, or was, or ever more will be, for wisdom speaks from out of the highest plane of infinite living mind. Man is a thought of Allah, all thoughts of Allah are infinite, they are not measured up by time, for things that are concerned with time begin and end. The thoughts of Allah are from the everlasting of the past unto the never-ending days to come. So is man, the original man. Nevertheless, operate as every other thought of Allah was but a seed, a seed that held within itself the potencies of Allah, just as the seed of any plant of earth holds deep within itself the attributes of that special plant. So the original man, as seed of Allah held deep within himself the attributes of every part of Allah. Now seeds are perfect, yea as perfect as the source from which they come, but they are not unfolded into life made manifest. The child in utero is perfect as the mother is.

So man, the seed must be deep planted in a soil that he might grow, unfold, as does the bud unfold to show the flower. The Asiatic seed that came forth from the heart of God Allah was full ordained to be the lord of the plane of soul and of the plane of things made manifest. So Allah, the husbandman of every thing that is, threw forth this Asiatic seed into the soil of soul, it grew apace, and man became a living soul and he became the lord of all the kingdom of the soul. Hark now, let every creature heat, the plane of soul is but the ether on the mental plane vibrating not so fast and in the slower rhythm of this plane, the essences of life are manifest, the per-fumes and the odor, the true sensations and all of love are manifest. These soul attributes become a body beautiful. A multitude of lessons man must learn upon the plane of soul and here he tarries many ages until his lessons are all learned.

Upon the boundary of the plane of soul the ether began to vibrate slower still and then the essences took on a garb, the perfumes and the odor and the true sensations and all of love were clothed in flesh and man was clothed in flesh. Perfected man must fall through all the ways of life, and so a carnal nature was full manifest, a nature that sprang forth from fleshly things. Without a foe, a soldier never knows his strength and thought must be developed by the exercise of strength. This carnal nature soon became a foe that man must fight, that he might be the strength of God Allah made manifest. Let life stand still and hear! Man is the master of all the plane of manifests, of protoplast, of mineral, of plant, of beast, but he has given up his birthright just to gratify his lower self, his carnal self. Nevertheless, the original man will full regain his lost estate, his heritage, but he must do it in a conflict that cannot be told in words. Yea he must suffer trials and temptations manifold, but let him know that cherubim and seraphim that rule the stations of the sun and the Mind of the mighty God, who rules the solar stars are his protectors and his guides, for this is his higher self and they will lead to victory the original man who is God. Man will be fully saved; redeemed, perfected by the things he suffers on the plane of flesh and on the plane of soul.

When man has conquered carnal things of the world his garb of flesh will then have served its purpose well and it will fall and will be no more. Then he will stand with his five bodies untrammeled on the plane of soul where he must full complete his victories. Unnumbered foes will stand before the man upon the plane of soul; there he must overcome them, every one. Thus knowledge, wisdom and understanding will ever be his beacon light, there is no failure for the original family, for the five on the left and the two on the right are leading on the victory. The Asiatic man cannot die, man the Mind is one and this is understanding the culture, thus man and Allah are one. When man has conquered every foe upon the plane of soul the seed will have full opened out and will have unfolded the Holy Breath. The grab of soul will then have served her purpose well and returned to the universe then man will need it never more and it will be space, this is triple darkness. Man and the Womb of man will then attain unto the blessedness of perfection and man will be the Mind and the universe will be Mental. While All is in The all, it is equally true that The all is in All. To He or Her who truly understands this truth hath come great Knowledge. The Universe is Mental held in the Mind of THE ALL. In the words of the 'Noble Prophet Drew Ali' as taught to the Asiatic Americans in the wilderness of North America all right peace. Bare witness that 120 lessons is strength to ones growth and developments once properly analyze, there are many introductions to root knowledge though hidden symbols that must be deciphered through intensive and diligent study of 120 degrees. For example, we ran the devil into the caves of West-Asia in the year 9001. Mr. Yacub was birthed in the year 8,367. It took 600 years to make devil. Now 2,600 years before the birth of the Prophet Musa is 8,320. In the Year 9,000, this means the devils language and knowledge of thought ways and actions. Therefore, in the year 8,320 the thought to make devil was given unto Rebecca, the mother of Yacub and Esau the brother. The 80 years of a gap is the indoctrination period 8,920 - 9,000 = 80. The devil was born in 9,000 birthed through the womb 8,920. Occult means that which is hidden. Occultism, consequently, is the science of hidden forces and the art of subjecting such to the Asiatic Man's control. The word occult since it depends upon the experience of the speaker for what is hidden to one may be perceived by another is wholly arbitrary. Nevertheless, there is nothing supernatural, nothing that is not governed by natural laws. Above and below, all obey those by which they manifest and while these laws are un-comprehended, any phenomenon seems mysterious. Progression depends upon knowledge. Man's only progression here or hereafter must be founded on knowledge. Only through knowledge of himself and of the powers and forces by which he is environed can he expect to progress. All knowledge is based upon experience. Following nature is our safest pilot. We discover that the first glimmer of consciousness, that which foreshadows knowledge, is concerned with distinguishing the me from the not me. Consequently, no one can deny his own existence and from this undeniable premise, any correct system of philosophy must start. The consciousness of the thinker thus firmly established is a perception of relations. Evolution is thus observed to be in the direction of increased perception, which is to be moving toward greater consciousness. Therefore, as evolution continues, consciousness expands and as evolution advances toward infinity the perception increase until absolute, consciousness is approached. Knowledge is nevertheless gained by experience. Such an experience is of course mental rather than physical, Peace.

Man is God of himself, his environment and the universe in which he lives. All people, by the right of their birth, are the inheritors of what their ancestors before them have or the material they have acquired. We inherit the good and the bad, and the responsibility to continue what they have or correct the wrong. Either way we will be judged in our lives by what we do in accord with the history we have inherited. 'All knowledge is but a branch of worship and all worship is but a branch of abstinence, and all abstinence is but a branch of trust in God and neither limit nor a finite end'. Over the years, evidence has been uncovered challenging established notions of the origins of life on Earth. Such as Lerone Bennett Jr., Dr. Frances Cress Welsing, Drusilla Dunjee Houston, Savina Teubal, Lana Cantrell, Stanley Lane-Poole, and John G. Jackson etc., have changed the outlook of life for millions of people good and bad. Why did W.D. Fard teach Elijah Muhummed such things about the men, women and children of Earth? Are the Archaeological finds of the Hittite, Canaanite and other Ancient texts and tales increasingly confirming the accuracy of the references that men such as Drew Ali and Father Allah used as tools and proof of the customs of Antiquity? 'Let us make Adam in our image and after our likeness' we look into these things today in the Books of Great men and women, for let the people think for them-selves.

Chango~Oggun~Babalawo

As above, so below, this is what the people of Earth teach to all, as they learned it from the true and living God in the olden days, before the European had taken them from the land of Africa. Chango' is the patron of fire, thunder, and lighting an Orisha Dada is a brother of Chango' and the Elegun Chango' is Priest of Chango'. Alafina Crueco are titles of Chango' as Ajaba is another name of the Orisha Dada, the brother of Chango. The Orisha Aganyu' owns the volcano, and is the father of Chango. The food or one of the most favorite foods prepared for Chango are okra and cornmeal, and the ayan tree is sacred to Chango'. Batea is the bowl of wood where Chango's thunderstones are kept. As learned from the Religion Santeria, 'come and go in peace'. The most interesting and important aspects of the Yoruba culture are its religious practices. The deities known as Orishas are extraordinarily in their behavior. In Africa, their number exceeds 600. In Latin America, their numbers are around 25.

As members of African tribes were scattered throughout the Americas by slave traders, the religion was influenced by new surroundings. This brought great diversity into the magic and ceremonies. The rites vary with each tribe. In Haiti, we have the Fon, Nago, Kongo, Ibo, and Dahomeans. In Cuba, Puerto Rico and the Dominican Republic we have Yoruba, Bantu and Kongo. In Cuba where Santeria originated, Yoruba became known as Lucumi or friendship. In Sierra Leone, they are known as Aku. The Cuban Lucumi is influenced by the Catholic iconolatry of their Spanish masters. In their efforts to hide their magical and religious practices from the Spaniards, they identified their deities with the saints of the Catholic Church.

All of the Yoruba deities worshiped in Santeria have been identified with Catholic saints. Santeria is a mixture of the magical rites of Yoruba and traditions of the Catholic Church. Therefore, Santeria is magic and its roots are from the heart of Africa.
This resulted in a great deal of persecution from the Spaniards, which forced the slaves (POW) to cloak their religion, in secrecy, this secrecy never existed in Africa, but is still observed by the practitioners of Santeria today. Santeria is an earth religion, which has its roots in nature and natural forces. The Orishas are divided into two groups, the white or cool (Obatala, Osain, Orisha-Oko, Oshun and Yemaya) and the dark or hot (***Chango, Oggun and Oya***). God Almighty (Oloddumare) created the Universe. Everything is made of Ashe, and through Ashe, everything is possible. The Universe is divided into two camps good and evil. The Ajogun must be propitiated so that they leave us in peace, and the Orishas must be propitiated so that they remain with us and grant us their Ashe. Remember Blood is the essence of life and is not to be shed lightly. Today this is the Religion of more than a hundred million people in Latin America and the US, from New York too Florida and from Washington State too Texas, Peace and Love to all.

JOHN WYCLIF
Chapter 19*

What is the birth record of said nations other than Islam? Answer: <u>Buddhism is 35,000 years old and Christianity is 551 years old.</u> **(See WD Fard & T.H.E.M. 1930 - 1934)** If we subtract 551 years from the date in which the student enrollment was written, we would not arrive at the date in which Jesus Christ so-called returned to the essence, which would be more or less the date in which the Western world calendar records history.

Christianity supposedly is the teachings of Jesus Christ, in essence, Jesus taught freedom, justice and equality, and at the time the Student enrollment was written, Christianity should have been <u>1,935</u> years old and not 551 years old. **(<u>Why the difference in dates</u>?)** Subtracting 551 years from the time the student enrollment that was written <u>1932</u> gives us the date 1381. The Bible was translated into English and given to the common people in this year. Prior to this date, only certain individuals of nobility were the ones in possession of the Bible, written in Latin and French. John Wyclif took it upon himself to make the Bible a common Possession of all Christians in England in the language of all the people. From him comes the first English translation of the New Testament, while the Old Testament comes from his association with Nicholas of Hereford. When the first translation emerged, it became the object of violent controversy.

The translation was opposed and forbidden. Thus, the mass of people came into the possession of the Bible unknown to the Church, yet many manuscripts survived and were wide spread among the common people. In many of his books, one may discover immense attacks upon the papacy and the entire hierarchy of his time. In the summer of <u>1381</u> ace Wycliffe formulated his doctrine of the Lord's Supper in twelve short sentences, and made it a duty to advocate it everywhere. Then the English hierarchy proceeded against him. The chancellor of the University of Oxford had some of the declarations pronounced heretical. When this fact was announced to Wycliffe, he declared that no one could change his convictions. He then appealed neither to the pope nor to the ecclesiastical authorities of the land, but to the king. He published his great confession upon the subject and a second writing in English intended for the common people. His pronouncements were no longer limited to the classroom they spread to the masses. The followers of John Wycliffe, the Lollards, grew greatly in number throughout the land. In the midst of this commotion came <u>the Peasants' Revolt of 1381</u>. Although Wycliffe disapproved of the revolt, he was blamed. Yet his friend and protector John of Gaunt, was the most hated by the rebels, and where Wycliffe's influence was greatest, the uprising found the least support. While in general the aim of the revolt was against the spiritual nobility, this came about because they were nobles, not because they were churchmen. Wycliffe's old enemy, Courtenay, now Archbishop of Canterbury, called (1382) an ecclesiastical assembly of notables at London.

During the consultations an earthquake occurred (May 21); the participants were terrified and wished to break up the assembly, but Courtenay declared the earthquake a favorable sign that meant the purification of the earth from erroneous doctrine.

On <u>Nov. 18, 1382,</u> Wycliffe was summoned before a synod at Oxford; he appeared, though apparently broken in body in consequence of a stroke, but determined. He still commanded the favor of the court and of parliament, to which he addressed a memorial. He was neither excommunicated then, nor deprived of his position. 'While Wycliffe was in the parish church on Holy Innocents' Day, <u>Dec. 28, 1384</u>, 'he again suffered a stroke, and was carried out the side-door of his church, in his chair'. John Wycliffe died on the last day of the year, three days later. The Council of Constance declared Wycliffe <u>(on May 4, 1415)</u> a stiff-necked heretic and under the ban of the Church. It was decreed that his books be burned and his remains be exhumed. This last did not happen until twelve more years later, when at the command of Pope Martin V they were dug up, burned, and the ashes cast into the river Swift that flows through Lutterworth.

THE HISTORY OF BUDDHA AS TAUGHT BY A SON OF FATHER ALLAH
Chapter 20

Buddha is an Original Asiatic man who was a Doctor, Physics and Mathematician. He set out to build a Nation in India, in the year <u>5,020 of the 23rd Qur'an</u>. His followers were wise but when Buddha died, they began to do other then the teachings of Buddha. The wall or gates of Mecca was built in the six thousandth year of the 24th Qur'an in order to keep the Buddhist Monks out, and they are the ones, who strayed away from Buddhism and Buddha, to change his testimony to make it easy on themselves. This only made them go astray, causing them to fight and kill one another in India as the Devil did to the original man in Mecca thousands of years later. One year a Minister of the scholarship clan under the first Buddha, who had been studying in Mecca visited India and the true followers of Buddha, he told them of the Monks and high Priestesses of the faraway land Mecca and how he taught that all men are Allah, and how He Allah had made Angles and Suns. Thus, Buddha would return from the dead as he did and would be praised as one of the Sons of Men who are Gods. Many tried to get into the city and take it from the true sons of Buddha; the students of the fallen Angels told the people that they would send four billion warriors from the Far East if they did not surrender the city over to the fallen Angels and their students. However, they did not fall for the tricks of the fallen Angels in that day and time.

Allah commissioned the Monks of Buddha to go and search for the new Buddha, who would return to the sons of men, but they were unable to find this one, so they all agreed that they would return to the temple and wait for this son of man to come. Many Monks became wild for they had started worshipping idols as gods, the truthful followers of Buddha stayed in India, but the Monks were ran out, of the city, this is why you have many versions of Buddha's teachings.

Buddha

1. What does Buddha mean? Buddha means the enlightened one, who has found their self, has therefore found the Universe and has been enlightened to the absolute truth.
2. When was the First Buddha born on this Earth, and who was he? Buddha was born <u>35,000</u> years ago and he was a Prophet of Allah.

3. When and where was Buddha born? Buddha was born in a place called Asia (Earth) in what is now called or known today as Pakistan India, therefore Buddha was of the Asiatic (Black man) descendent and was not what is considered oriental.

4. Is Buddha's name written in the Book of Life? Yes! He was a God not a Buddhist, just as Jesus was a God and not a Christian.

5. Who gave Buddha his name? Allah himself gave Buddha his name at the age of 30 he was educated by the greatest scientists of Asiatic nation in that day and time.

6. When did Buddha leave India in that day and time? The Date is unknown.

7. What did Buddha look like? Buddha was very dark in complexion, with dark brown-planted eyes, with curly dark brown hair he was an original man.

8. What are Buddha's teachings? Buddha taught Freedom, Justice and Equality!

9. 35,000 years ago means 5,020 in the 23rd Qur'an, each cycle or Qur'an equals 25,000 years.

10. In the year 15,020 in the 24th Qur'an or cycle is 1934 ace.

Gautama Buddha

On this day, Buddhists celebrate the commemoration of the birth of Gautama Buddha, thought to have lived in India from 563 BCE to 483 BCE Actually, the Buddhist tradition that celebrates his birthday on April 8th originally placed his birth in the 11th century BC, and it was not until the modern era that scholars determined that he was more likely born in the sixth century BC, and possibly in May rather than April according to the Tripitaka, Gautama Buddha was born as Prince Siddhartha, the son of the king of the Sakya people. The kingdom of the Sakyas was situated on the borders of present-day Nepal and India. Siddhartha's family was of the Gautama clan. His mother, Queen Mahamaya, gave birth to him in the park of Lumbini, in what is now southern Nepal. A pillar placed there in commemoration of the event by an Indian emperor in the third century BC still stands. At his birth, it was predicted that the prince would become either a great world monarch or a Buddha (a supremely enlightened teacher). The Brahmans told his father, King-Suddhodana, that Siddhartha would become a ruler if he were kept isolated from the outside world. The king took pains to shelter his son from misery and anything else that might influence him toward the religious life.

Siddhartha was brought up in great luxury, and he married and fathered a son. At age 29, he decided to see more of the world and began excursions off the palace grounds in his chariot. In successive trips, he saw an old man, a sick man, and a corpse, and since he had been protected from the miseries of aging, sickness, and death, his charioteer had to explain what they were.

Finally, Siddhartha saw a monk, and, impressed with the man's peaceful demeanor, he decided to go into the world to discover how the man could be so serene in the midst of such suffering. Siddhartha secretly left the palace and became a wandering ascetic. He traveled south, where the centers of learning were, and studied meditation under the teachers Alara Kalama and Udraka Ramaputra. He soon mastered their systems, reaching high states of mystical realization, but was unsatisfied and went out again in search of nirvana, the highest level of enlightenment. For nearly six years, he undertook fasting and other austerities, but these techniques proved ineffectual and he abandoned them. After regaining his strength, he seated himself under a tree at what is now in west-central India and promised not to rise until he had attained the supreme enlightenment.

After fighting off Mara, an evil spirit who tempted him with worldly comforts and desires, Siddhartha reached enlightenment, becoming a Buddha at the age of 35. The Gautama Buddha then traveled to the deer park near Benares, India, where he gave his first sermon and outlined the basic doctrines of Buddhism. According to Buddhism, there are "four noble truths", existence is suffering; this suffering is caused by human craving; there is a cessation of the suffering, which is nirvana; and nirvana can be achieved, in this or future lives, though the "eight-fold path" of right views, right resolve, right speech, right action, right livelihood, right effort, right mindfulness and right concentration. For the rest of his life, the Buddha taught and gathered disciples to his Sangha, or community of monks. He died at age 80, telling his monks to continue working for their spiritual liberation by following his teachings. Gautama's form of Buddhism eventually spread from India to Central and Southeast Asia, China, Korea, Japan, and, in the 20th century, to the West. **(See Chapter 19 of this book)**

JOHN HARDY HAWKINS JR.
Chapter 21

The spread of the Culture I-God had stopped to complete the ruling of the Europeans after they had over-populated Europe, Allah allowed them to spread out. He gave a guide to lead them; Columbus was a half-original man. He guided them over to the new world, for Allah had told Moses one of there, kind would guide them all the way. They realized the country would have to be built up and they knew they could not build up the country for they were not strong enough. Their Queen, Elizabeth, called in leaders and world travelers and wanted to know, if there existed a people on the face of the planet earth who could stand the hard work and yet be submissive enough to submit to the task. John Hawkins told them yes, there are, along the Nile, the strongest people and the wisest that ever lived yet, they had never been lied to. The Queen appointed John Hawkins the job of getting them into the United States of America. This was called the hundred-year plan. John Hawkins one day sailed along the Nile. He came among the tribe of Shabazz. He was flying a red flag, which represented Freedom, and his ship was named Jesus, which means justice. He came among the tribe of Shabazz offering them peace. Our people never being lied to or mislead, accepted his greetings and him as a brother. He lived among us for 29-1/2 years, learning our customs, our way of life, our culture, our philosophy, our tongue, everything he could about us. After learning all he could he started a rumor about a land to the west of milk and honey, a paradise, a place of plenty. Our people were living along the Nile River; the children were allowed to play with diamonds of such size as to be astonishing. They were advanced and played with algebra as a game and past time play. We gave out high mathematics and advanced astronomy. We were advanced in arts and mastered all seven sciences of the planet earth. We were the most beautiful people physically one had ever laid eyes on, because we had mastered the sciences of proper eating and caring for the body. We could outwork any people on the planet and could endure hardship longer than anyone else could.

Yet we are the most devoted and the most mathematical people, we are (Father) Allah's choice, his most beloved sons and daughters. We are his perfect example for our brothers and sisters. A house of presents and holy ones, we are (Job), Allah's most faithful servants, we are royal and holy and Allah, to whom we are one completely with as God. We know every inch of the planet, but when the rumor started we fell for it, prophecy had to be fulfilled, we went aboard John Hawkins's ship and this was to discuss the place and get a better picture of it and better understanding. While everyone was preparing, the hatch was closed and the ship was allowed to drift into the sea. When day light came, they were on their way. The men became aware and some were successful in going overboard but most were outnumbered and subdued.

POLYGAMY IN AMERICA
Chapter 22

There is a misconception about the Bible prohibiting polygamy. The Bible allows polygamy in both the Old Testament and the New Testament. A brief look at polygamy in the Bible let us look at some of the verses from the Old Testament, which allows polygamy: In Exodus 21:10, a man can marry an infinite amount of women without any limits to how many he can marry. In second Samuel 5:13 first Chronicles 3:1-9, 14:3, King David had six wives and numerous concubines. In first Kings 11:3, King Solomon had 700 wives and 300 concubines. In second Chronicles 11:21, King Solomon's son Jeroboam had 18 wives and 60 concubines. In Deuteronomy, 21:15 "If a man has two wives, and he loves one but not the other and both bear him sons...." There are a lot more verses from the Old Testament that allow polygamy, but I think that the above are sufficient to prove my point. Jesus said, "Do not think that I have come to abolish the Law or the Prophets; I have not come to abolish them but to fulfill them. I tell you the truth, until heaven and earth disappear, not the smallest letter, not the least stroke of a pen; will by any means disappear from the Law until everything is accomplished. (Matthew 5:17-18) Christians always say, oh this law does not exist in the New Testament; it is only the Old Testament.

Well, according to Matthew 5:17-18 above, we clearly see that Jesus honored the Old Testament, and forces Christians to follow the unmodified laws of it that have not been replaced by newer ones in the New Testament. The Old Testament as we clearly see above does indeed allow polygamy without any doubt! There is not a single verse from the New Testament that prohibits polygamy. Christians usually mistakenly present the following verses from the Bible to prove that polygamy in the New Testament is not allowed:

1. Matthew 19:1-12 "1. When Jesus had finished saying these things, he left Galilee and went into the region of Judea to the other side of the Jordan.
2. Large crowds followed him, and he healed them there.
3. Some Pharisees came to him to test him. They asked, "Is it lawful for a man to divorce his wife for any and every reason?"

4. "Haven't you read," he replied, "that at the beginning the Creator `made them male and female,'

5. He said, `for this reason a man will leave his father and mother and be united to his wife, and the two will become one flesh'?

6. So they are no longer two, but one. Therefore what God has joined together, let man not separate."

7. "Why then," they asked, "did Moses command that a man give his wife a certificate of divorce and send her away?"

8. Jesus replied, "Moses permitted you to divorce your wives because your hearts were hard. Nevertheless, it was not this way from the beginning.

9. I tell you that anyone who divorces his wife, except for marital unfaithfulness, and marries another woman commits adultery."

10. The disciples said to him, "If this is the situation between a husband and wife, it is better not to marry."

11. Jesus replied, "Not everyone can accept this word, but only those to whom it has been given.

12. For, some are eunuchs because they were born that way; others were made that way by men; and others have renounced marriage because of the kingdom of heaven. The one who can accept this should accept it." Polygamy may be abhorrent to most Americans, but in the global community, it is common, normal and accepted. 'Although the percentage of men in the world who have more than one wife is relatively small, as many as a third of the world's population belongs to a community that allows it,' there are many plural marriages in Africa, the Middle East and in Asia. The ancient Hebrews, as portrayed in the Old Testament, clearly believed in multiple partnerships and God nowhere condemns this practice. The very first marriage, Adam and Eve, in many ways serves as a prototype, if you will. Notice that God knew that it was not good that Adam is alone and God provided for Adam a "help meet" (counter part that was a complement to Adam, Gen. 2: 18). Observe how God did not simply provide another man, but for Adam God made woman, the "glory of the man" (Gen. 2:18, I Cor.11:7). Hence, same sex marriage is not part of God's arrangement for the marriage bond. Humankind has practiced polygamy for thousands of years. Many of the ancient Israelites were polygamous, some having hundreds of wives.

In the Bible, King Solomon is said to have had seven hundred wives and three hundred concubines. King David (Dawud) had ninety-nine wives and Jacob (Yacub) had four. Early society had not put any restrictions on the number of wives a man could or should have in Africa this is a European way of life. Jesus was not known to have spoken against polygamy. As recent as the 17th century, polygamy was practiced and accepted by the Christian Church. The Mormons (Church of Jesus Christ of the Latter Day Saints) has allowed and practiced polygamy in the United States.

Monogamy was introduced into Christianity at the time of Paul when many revisions took place in Christianity. This was done in order for the church to conform to the Greco-Roman culture where men were monogamous but owned many slaves who were free for them to use: in other word, unrestricted polygamy. Early Christians invented ideas that women were "full of sin" and man was better off to "never marry." Since this would be the end of humankind, these same people compromised and said, "Marry only one."

Many times in the modern societies when relations are strained, the husband simply deserts his wife. Then he cohabits with a prostitute or other immoral woman without marriage.

Actually, there are three kinds of polygamy practiced in Western societies

Serial polygamy, that is, marriage, divorce, marriage, divorce and so on any number of times. A man married to one woman but having and supporting one or more mistresses. An unmarried man having a number of mistresses, Islam condones polygamy. Wars cause the number of women to exceed the number of men. In a monogamous society these women, left without husbands or support, and resort to prostitution, illicit relationships with married men resulting in illegitimate children with no responsibility on the part of the father, or lonely unmarried women or widowhood. Some Western men take the position that monogamy protects the rights of women. However, are these men really concerned about the rights of women? The society has many practices that exploit and suppress women, leading to women's liberation movements from the suffragettes of the early twentieth century to the feminists of today. The truth of the matter is that monogamy protects men, allowing them to "play around" without responsibility. Easy birth control and easy legal abortion has opened the door of illicit sex to women and she has been lured into the so-called sexual revolution. Nevertheless, she is still the one who suffers the trauma of abortion and the side effects of birth control methods.

Taking aside the plagues of venereal disease, herpes and AIDS, the male continues to enjoy himself free of worry. Men are the ones protected by monogamy while women continue to be victims of men's desires. Polygamy is very much opposed by the male dominated society because it would force men to face up to responsibility and fidelity. It would force them to take responsibility for their polygamous inclinations and would protect and provide for women and children. The countries where polygamy is illegal, large number of people practice extra-marital sex or live with a mistress. The number of mistress may go up to a dozen or so.

The Western society and the church have closed their eyes to this particular sinful act in their own country and criticize Muslim countries for polygamy. "If you fear that you will not deal fairly by the orphans, marry of the women, who seem good to you, two or three or four; but if you fear that you shall not be able to deal justly with them, then only one or one that your right hands possess. That will be more suitable, to prevent you from doing injustice." (Qur'an 4:3) The Qur'an allows a man to marry more than one woman but only if he can deal justly with them. "You will never be able to deal justly between wives however much you desire (to do so). But (if you have more than one wife) do not turn altogether away (from one), leaving her as in suspense." (Qur'an 4:129)

Melchisedek

The King of Righteousness is a man who led the worship in the sacred tent or in the temple and who offered sacrifices to the one God. Some of the more important priests are "chief priests," and the most important priest is the "high priest." For this

Melchisedek said that; Christ is a High Priest forever after the order of Melchisedek, King of Salem, priest of the most high God, who met Abraham returning from the slaughter of the kings, and blessed him; To whom also Abraham gave a tenth part of all; first being by interpretation King of righteousness, and after that also King of Salem, which is, King of peace; Without father, without mother, without descent, having neither beginning of days, nor end of life; but made like unto the Son of God; abided as a priest continually. Now consider how great this man was, unto whom even the patriarch Abraham gave the tenth of the spoils. Verily they that are of the sons of Levi, who receive the office of the priesthood, have a commandment to take tithes of the people according to the law, that is, of their brethren though they come out of the loins of Abraham. However, he whose descent from them received tithes of Abraham, and blessed him that had the promises. Moreover, without all contradiction the less is blessed of the better. One of the greatest men who ever lived was Melchisedek. This King of Righteousness and Peace is one of most admired and honored men representing the dignity of God. Many Jewish historians thought he was Shem, since in their eyes there could not have been anyone more respected than Abram. Many Bible commentators believed that Melchisedek was either Jesus Christ or an angel, because Hebrews 7:3 mentions that he had no father or mother; and his beginning and end were not known. When a man is in daily commune with God and is, living a clean life God speaks to him the mysteries of life and the kingdom of God. God reveals to this individual his detailed plan and purpose, so he can conquer any situation or circumstance. This person can respond to situations without the benefit of a written text. The nurturing of this timeless wisdom enabled Melchisedek to correctly do and say new things. Melchisedek became the man of many firsts. Genesis 14:18-19 Melchizedek, king of Salem, brought out bread and wine, and being a priest of God Most High, he blessed Abram with these words: Blessed be Abram by God Most High, the creator of heaven and earth. In addition, Melchisedek King of Salem brought forth bread and wine: 'and he was the priest of the Most High. Moreover, he blessed him, and said, blessed be Abram of the Most High, possessor of heaven and earth. Faith comes by hearing, and, specifically, by hearing the Word of God.'

This Word must be delivered by a skilled and anointed preacher sent from God. Even though Abram was the father of faith, he needed someone to teach him faith in God. Melchisedek was fully equipped to teach him faith. Abram had just won a major battle and had recovered Lot, the people, and their possessions. In the midst of this victory, he encountered a man who will affect his life forever. Melchisedek instituted the serving of the first communion with bread and wine. Abram means the father of height, stature, and elevation. In the ancient days, Lucifer wanted to be more that a leader he wanted to be God, the leader for all to serve. Melchisedek taught him about El-Hellion. The Canaanite word "El" means Elohim, IHVH is the first clause of everything; He is the possessor of heaven and earth, the Almighty and Everlasting God.

IRS
Chapter 23

Now we come to a very important part of this book, the story of the IRS, a piece of the puzzle to America. In 1913, just thirty days before he was set to leave office, the U.S.

Secretary of State, Philander Knox, declared by his certification that the proposed Amendment had been legally and properly ratified by 3/4ths of the state legislatures, despite the well documented fact that he had been informed by his solicitor general that the Amendment had not come close to being ratified. Then Congress adopted the 16th Amendment to the US Constitution. Within months of the declaration by Knox, Congress crafted and passed the Income Tax Act of 1913, which included a definition of income, that stretched the meaning of the legal term income well beyond the constitutional meaning and well beyond the documented intent of the European framers of the Amendment, as recorded in every official and professional document of the era: the Congressional Record, congressional committee reports, law reviews, journals of political science, newspapers of record and so forth. With its statutory, definition of income, Congress improperly broadened the definition of income to include money received by a person in direct exchange for that person's labor. In technical terms, Congress included a non-apportioned, direct tax on the salaries, wages and compensation of all American workers. Even though the Act exempted from the tax those workers earning less than $4,000, the government soon began to receive so much money from the income tax that its revenue increased from about $380 million in 1914 to more than $3.7 billion by 1918. The Income Tax Act of 1913 also instituted withholding at the source and the tax return, Form 1040. The-income Tax Act of 1913 provided the government with a stream of revenue that enabled it to spend large amounts of money before it had it. The central government not only had much more money to spend, it could now do whatever it wanted to do, even if it did not have the money to do it. 'The Income Tax Act of 1913' enabled the government to pledge, as collateral, the labor of its citizens to secure its debt. The government could now guarantee the repayment of borrowed money by forcefully taking bread from the mouths of labor. However, the still-standing Constitution prohibited a tax on labor. The Income Tax Act of 1913 was soon tested in Court. In 1916, the Supreme Court brought the unconstitutional labor tax to a screeching halt.

The Supreme Court ruled in Brushaber v. Union Pacific, 240 U.S.1 and the cases bundled with it, including Stanton v Baltic Mining Co., 240 US 103, that wages are not income within the meaning of the income tax Amendment to the Constitution, or any other provision of the Constitution. The Supreme Court's decision in Brushaber soundly rejected the government's self-interested interpretation of the definition of income within the meaning of the Constitution, and specifically limited to whom" and where the income tax could apply. The Brushaber court explicitly concluded that the16th Amendment gave Congress no new powers of taxation, meaning that direct taxes on wages, salaries and compensation received by workers in direct exchange for their labor fell outside of the meaning of the 16th Amendment and still must satisfy the fundamental requirement of apportionment as a direct tax, if, indeed, the government could overcome the slavery issue. The Brushaber decision forced Congress to consider changing the statutory definition of income, to bring it in line with the Constitution.

However, true to form and consistent with the nature of governmental power, the government was loathe to relinquish the spoils and booty that flowed from its direct tax on labor, and the power and control that came with the tax and its enforcement mechanisms the IRS. The crime continued in the halls of Congress and in the White House with the adoption of the Income Tax Act of 1916 Amended in 1917. Although the 1916 Act ended withholding of wages, salaries and compensation and ordered the money that had been withheld from workers to be returned to those workers, and the Treasury Secretary issued Treasury Directive 2635 and saw to it that the money withheld was returned, the 1916 Act failed to define the legal term income.

While the act carried over the definition of income from the 1913 Act, Congress specifically qualified in Section 25 of the Act that the income subject to the 1913 Act was not the same income to be taxed under the 1916 Act. No further explanation was provided in the Act. In other words, after the Supreme Court's explicit ruling in Brushaber, the government adopted a revised tax law that said, in effect, the meaning of the word income has changed but we are not going to tell you how. Confused or ignorant of the law, and too patriotic and engaged with World War I to question their government, workers toiling above the $4,000 exemption level kept sending in their Form 1040 and paying a tax on money earned by them in direct exchange for their own labor. As the years went on, the tax rates went up, the exemptions dropped, and more Americans succumbed to the popular belief that the law required them to file and pay. During the great Depression, the crime deepened.

While the more wealthy workers were unwittingly continuing to pay a tax on money earned in direct exchange for their labor, not just on their passive income, Congress and the President, again acted without constitutional authority, and in defiance of the now numerous and consistent rulings of the United States Supreme Court the latest ruling coming in 1920 in Eisner v Macomber, 252 U.S. 189. In 1933, the government adopted a law forcing all workers to pay an income tax by another name, on money earned in direct exchange for their own labor. The new labor tax was called a Social Security tax. Along with this new labor tax, withholding was instituted in America. During World War II, the crime deepened further.

Once again, in defiance of the Constitution and the rulings of the Supreme Court, the Congress and the President instituted still another labor tax on all Americans, not just the wealthy, calling it a, 'Victory Tax'. Along with the 'Victory Tax' came withholding of the 'Victory Tax' at the source. Drunk with power, taking advantage of the People during times of strife, the government was piling on one direct labor tax after another, calling them 'income taxes', without ever statutorily defining the term 'income'. The 'Victory Tax' was a tax on the money people earned in direct exchange for their own labor. The People were told that 'Victory Tax' would expire with the conclusion of the War. It did not. Neither did withholding. The Victory Tax continued unabated, becoming the Federal Income Tax of today, in 1965, the crime deepened even further.

Once again, in defiance of the Constitution and the rulings of the Supreme Court, the Congress and the President piled on yet another direct tax on the labor of all working men and women, calling it a Medicare Tax. Along with the 'Medicare Tax' came withholding of the 'Medicare Tax' at the source. Since 1916, Congress and the Executives, with the cooperation of the lesser courts, have been relentlessly tightening the yoke of slavery on all Americans as they have imposed and enforced an increasing number of unconstitutional direct taxes on the salaries, wages and compensation of Asiatics and Europeans alike. Beyond this, the institutions of government have, by duplicity, threat and force, coerced the businesses of America into collecting these labor taxes by withholding them at the source, the paychecks of American workers. A tax on labor regardless of its label or beneficent intent is a 'slave tax,' and is a violation of not only the fundamental rights of labor, but it is patently unconstitutional. Most Asiatic and European Americans, covered with a blanket of propaganda, believe they are free as they pledge allegiance to this country, a Republic, but follow the dictates of a government run by elected and appointed officials whose first allegiance is to their Party. Make no mistake: money earned in direct exchange for labor is being seized by the government, without rightful authority, from the workers of America, by force that is, by violence to be distributed, with its opportunities for profit, influence and corruption among the elected and appointed public officials and party workers, and those that seek to keep them in office for their own benefit.

The Cover-Up

Americans who know the truth about the 'income tax', and who protest the labor tax and government's continuing retaining of their money, are dragged first through an administrative process and then, if necessary through a civil and/or criminal judicial process all of which suffer from fatal Due Process defects because there can be no law authorizing a tax on labor.

Licensing

The authority of licensing is the power to control, regulate, stifle, intimidate, rob and or destroy an individual or an organization and their activities or products. Licensing is an ugly fist of protectionism suited better to a dictatorship than a free republic.
The boards and commissions whose function it is to oversee such things assure and protect the government's additional source of revenue. Tyrant governments prefer that their subjects (slaves) be required to ask permission prior to and as a condition for public private and or independent activities. These governments want servile subjects, who do what they are told, hence the necessity of creating an acceptance of licensing as being for the common good, or for public protection. These tyrant governments pass or raise servile subjects, rather than worthy free Constitutional citizens.

Article 1 section 8 wherein the congress was given the option to regulate through licensing commerce with foreign nations, among the states and with 'Indian tribes'. The constitution itself is a contract of limitations on the U.S. government.

The Constitution is a prescription for exactly what the U.S. government shall do and how it may proceed. Government licensing creates injustice and makes the blessings at tranquility and liberty insecure. Government licensing is centered on rights and privileges. It is a right to have safe passage, be self-governed as a free man; an individual of the U.S.A. may elect to do anything, so long as there is no threat to the life, liberty or property of another individual. We the Free Asiatics, who are Moors, Gods and Earths, have the right to claim our Constitution. That is our right as free people and no permission is needed to exercise that right.

SUPREME MATHEMATICS
Chapter 24

These lessons were give to the 5% from the Father in 1964, every one who received these lessons had to learn how to quote each degree before they could move on to the next number. This is some of what the Father taught his children from 1964 to 1969.

(1) Knowledge is to know, listen and observe, Knowledge as a body of accumulated facts. Knowledge is the foundation for all things in existence, as the sun is the foundation for our solar system and man is the foundation for his family.

(2) Wisdom is the manifestation of ones knowledge, the ways and actions one uses to make his or her knowledge, to know truth. Such as speaking wisely to the wise, to the dumb, or to possess a wise mind, Wisdom is the woman.

(3) Understanding is the mental picture one draws of knowledge, wisdom. To see things much clearer for what they are, visible through the all - Seeing Eye that is the mind. Understanding is the child.

(4) Culture or Freedom, culture is ones way of life. Islam is the culture of freedom and righteousness, the culture of peace in which all things coincide and live in harmony.

(5) Power or Refinement, power is the truth. Truth in origin only means of refinement; to go according to the truth is to make ones self-known again. Truth is the power to resurrect the mentally dead from their present state of unawareness and ignorance of self.

(6) Equality means to be equal in all aspects of ones true self.

(7) God is the Original Man, the All and all is the Creator Allah. I is self, self is the true reality son man God (Allah). **(A mans' ideal is his God as man unfolds, his God unfolds)**

(8) Build or destroy; build means to add on to life a positive creation or education. Destroy means to know of, take that which is untrue and add light to the knowledge.

(9) Born is to bring into existence mental birth of self.

(0) Cipher is the completion of a circle, 360°.

9 Reasons why Allah-U-Akbar

This is a lesson that was given out to the Gods & Earths in (Medina) Brklyn NY; you were required to quote the lesson before you could go on to the next degree and or lesson from Father Allah of the 5% Nation. This is an Introduction to one of the 5% Nations

Books of Life.

1. Allah's knowledge is supreme, unequaled by any other god, Allah is the knower and CREATOR of all things.

2. Allah's wisdom is infinite and purifies the brain of the Asiatic man, and creates an extension from God to Child.

3. Allah's understanding is supreme and has made all things easily understood, for understanding can answer any given question at any given time.

4. Allah's culture is purified ways and actions created with knowledge and understanding. Culture is education, which Allah completes with no beginning, or ending, I do not deny myself for my culture is ISLAM since my culture is that of GOD ALLAH. He will be praised forever in my presence.

5. Power for Allah's supreme power of the mind is the highest form of life that can be conceived and lived by Allah, man's power is knowledge, understanding manifested with 7.5 oz. of brain.

6. For there is none equal to Allah (God); Allah teaches equality is the 110° in 120°, For God Allah deals in equality with all creations.

7. ALLAH being the seventh wonder of the ancient world, the Godhead is the creator and teaches by the pinhead, that which Muhammad knew. Goddess is God less than man. *{(YX) + (XX) = LIFE}*

8. The Universal builder are the Gods who build unity of the mind and the neurons nerve—cells and destroy the arch sinners in hell. Allah saved the Gods and Earths from the unknown destruction and reconstructed the most dynamic and powerful nation on earth.

9. Born to give to Gods his own self, which Allah did when born to supreme maturity of a divine idea, which is the thought in the Mind. This is self-completion of beginning to the end. Now God's life did not start at a beginning or have an end, that was what was created between Aleph A OX; and the Tau, Th, The original man is the only one to go from knowledge to born without going through the womb of the earth. Knowledge to born was manifested mentally first then in a physical sense.

SUPREME ALPHABETS
Chapter 25

1. A. Allah is the Supreme Being, the Asiatic man from Asia. God of the Universe, Lord of All the Worlds from the highest to the Lowest. The original man, the giver and taker of life, the foundation of all life, the father of reality and the knowledge of the sun, the following diagram shows the complete realm (cipher) of the Asiatic man's body, keeps everything pure, true and living; blanket of protection 5 x 72 = 360. The power of God's wisdom shows forth his understanding of his equality added onto his cipher. A-Arm = 72, L-Leg = 72, L-Leg = 72, A-Arm = 72, H-Head = 72.

2. B. Be or Born is the realm or state of being horn into existence. Born is to be aware of everything because everything is from the Sun, Moon and Stars; Man, Woman and Child; past, present and future. Born is to be complete and to give birth to wisdom. Knowing that everything is real, one must born his or her knowledge to show wisdom to be real.

3. C. See is to knowledge wisdom being born and gain a clear picture that will be the understanding. To see is to he equipped with sight; both insight and eyesight; "C" is also the cream.

4. D. Divine is knowledge and wisdom being understood, showing its completion and manifesting a perfect state of existence equating the culture which is God the Divine being, Divine being that which is sacred.

5. E. Equality is to be equal with all society and nations of the earth, showing and proving with the power of equality that we are the fathers of civilization, also, to equal all nations with the science of education, equality is the woman.

6. F. Father, the original man Fat-her with knowledge, wisdom and understanding of life. Father of the Five Percent Nation, Father Allah.

7. G. God is being himself at all times, knowledge equality born God, dealing equal with the knowledge known to Allah, Supreme Being, Man is God and the Asiatic Mind is self. (IHVH, Allah, TaHo)

8. H. He or Her is the man or woman who has knowledge of self and is building a strong foundation. He who is God; she who is the Earth, the woman planet to bring about the Gods and Earths and teach them at birth, He or Her without the knowledge of self cannot build but only destroy and or take many other lives.

9. I. Islam/I is self and self is the true reality son of man is God. Woman is earth and life when advocated for the same cause, to be reborn into the knowledge of self (I-self-lord-and-master).

10. J. Justice is the star, meaning your reward, regardless of whether it is one of happiness or sorrow. These are rewards and/or penalties. In addition, knowledge added to the cipher, REWARD - Just-I-C-Equality with which I have been blessed, PENALTY - Just-ice to be frozen at 32 degrees.

11. K. King, God is the King of kings meaning that God is the only King there is. Ruler of a kingdom, the equivalent of God himself, Father and He, The King rules because he is wise and just. One who knows the ledge for his word is life. In the beginning was the word and the word is GOD.

12. L. Love Hell or Right (LORD), love is the emotion that God blesses the woman with (in life). Many men and women possess this emotion and to those who have failed to cope with it, it has been proven to-be-a handicap.

Love to those who have gotten over this burden realize that love is understanding and not two separate qualities. Understanding brings on love or hate, love brings on understanding, hatred, can be caused by what you understand or do not understand. Those who have realized the truth of love have proven that he is a LORD. Lord is the equivalent of GOD, KING, HE, FATHER and thereby abides in paradise (heaven). Hell is the home of the ignorant, those who lack knowledge, of self. God shows his love by manifesting the Knowledge of' himself through his wisdom, which reveals the hell one must go through in order to be right, knowledge the wisdom to bring forth love (understanding).

13. M. Master is one who possesses 360 degrees of knowledge, wisdom and understanding. The equivalent of Lord, He, King, Father: God that is I, in addition, one

who knows the ledge of his understanding, enabling him to manifest the culture that is I-God, too knowledge understanding.

14. N. Now, (Nation), End, now is the time to get knowledge of self or end in a pit of ignorance. Nation the United Asiatic people dark and light, (Black, Brown, Red & Yellow) the pale person is in a race with time now to avoid the wrath of the Asiatic Nation (God). Knowledge the culture to show the power.

15. O. Cipher is a people, place or being, a circle that consists of 360 degrees or a cycle of life, C I Power Her, Her Power I C.

16. P. Power is strength, energy, magnetism. Truth is the ultimate power, star or child. Knowledge equality is God; therefore, knowledge itself is born equality.

17. Q. Queen is the woman factor of life. Mother or the womb of life, she is queen when she is doing the knowledge to God, this is to build or destroy, Queen is also equality wisdom.

18. R. Rule or Ruler (righteous, right, ruler) is a guide which God, the Asiatic man, uses to keep everything right and exact. Righteous are the Asiatic people according to nature. Right is the proper nature of things and people. Ruler is one who leads a king and/or queen when the King is not physically present.

19. S. Savior/Self is the one possessing the powers of God and resurrects all people after first saving self, one who saves all who want to be saved and add on to self. Self is the true reality of one, be it man or woman.

20. T. Truth or Square, truth understands the reality of wisdom cipher. God shows his powers and proves his powers, and presents the truth regardless of what angles of a square. Ninety degrees to each angle (4 x 90 = 360). The square is a multiple of four and the cube is a multiple of six.

21. U. Universe, the Universe is the home of the galaxies that is the home of our solar system. The universe owns and belongs to all Asiatic men and women. U and I verse the devil. You shall be pertaining to the woman when dealing in completing the home (child). You also is self, King, Savior, Queen, Her, Woman.

22. V. Victory is to obtain the knowledge, wisdom and understanding. A man that is blind, deaf and dumb has to take on the Seal of Victory to win.

23. W. Wisdom is wise words spoken by a wise man. This is power, when Allah speaks it is called wisdom, for when He speaks, it is like an ocean that would never go dry. Wisdom is the bridge to knowledge and understanding, wisdom is the woman.

24. X. Unknown is the identity of self, woman, man and God because people are not wise to their true culture (I God); X in genetics is the female factor or chromosome.

25. Y. Why, the question most asked to justify, why does he (the Uncle) like the devil? Why does the devil call our people African? Why are there so many of our people still dead? This is because of they do not accept the wisdom and power of God. In genetics, the male factor or chromosome is Y, God knowledge on the Y that has three points, foundation, right point and left point (peace).

26. Z. Zig, Zag, Zig is knowledge, wisdom and understanding. Zig and knowledge are alike and zag is un-a-like my self (peace).

In Conclusion, I say peace to all on this 28th day, in this first sign of the Zodiac, in the year 15078 AC (3/21/1992). This Book was manifested by Divine39A, Finished on 7/7/2007.

Peace and Love to all people of the planet Earth who want to know the truth of the so-called Black-man, woman and child, for they are the founders of civilization the world over. Peace!